THE NEW
TECHNOLOGY
STATE

www.amplifypublishinggroup.com

The New Technology State: How Our Digital Dreams Became Societal Nightmares—and What We Can Do About It

During the publishing process, some updates were made and some language clarified, as is normal. These changes were made solely by Mr. Raduchel.

For more information, please contact:
Amplify Publishing, an imprint of Amplify Publishing Group
620 Herndon Parkway, Suite 220
Herndon, VA 20170
info@amplifypublishing.com

Library of Congress Control Number: 2023901933
CPSIA Code: PRV0523A
ISBN-13: 978-1-63755-746-4
Printed in the United States

To the memory of
John Kenneth Galbraith

THE NEW TECHNOLOGY STATE

*How Our Digital Dreams Became
Societal Nightmares——
and What We Can Do About It*

BILL RADUCHEL

Evolved from 2019 conversations with
TOM TUGENDHAT

CONTENTS

Author's Note. 1

Introduction 5

1   The Age of the Algorithm. 13

2   Facebook's Angry Invisible Hand. 25

3   Data Is the New Oil 35

4   Halstead Length. 43

5   Answer-Seeking 63

6   Abstraction Layers 69

7   The Declining Relevance of Neoclassical Economics 81

8   Technology: Disrupter in Chief 95

9   Algorithmic Scale 109

10   The Social Rate of Discount. 123

11   The End of Privacy / The Rise of Surveillance 141

12   Media and Technology. 163

13   The New Politics 185

14   The New Technology State. 199

Conclusion: Where Do We Go Now? 213

Acknowledgments 227

Endnotes. 229

AUTHOR'S NOTE

The writing of this book began more than a decade ago in conversations with Tom Tugendhat at the Dialog Conference, a gathering of global thought leaders in tech, business, and academia.

We came to the conference from totally different pathways. I am an American tech executive who was fortunate to be present along the way as computer technology evolved from the back office to our hands. As these technologies evolved over the past sixty years, I interacted with the many personalities who shaped it. I evolved from a Harvard PhD in econometrics to a computer scientist at my perch at high-level positions at Data Resources, McGraw-Hill, Xerox, Sun Microsystems, AOL, AOL Time Warner, and Opera Software.

Tom started out as a British journalist in the Middle East, but his life was also shaped by the British Army as he served in combat during the Iraq War and in Afghanistan in both military and civilian roles. His latest role was as the military assistant to the UK's Chief of the Defence Staff before entering Parliament, where he became chair of the Foreign Affairs Committee and then Security Minister.

Despite widely different life experiences and training, in multiple conversations at Dialog we found much common ground on where the world was headed and the role of technology. As we continued those conversations, I remembered the prophetic words of the legendary economist John Kenneth Galbraith (with whom I'd worked closely at Harvard) in his landmark 1967 book *The New Industrial State*, which was the basis for the course we co-taught in its final years.

In the book, Galbraith examines the impact of the vastly more sophisticated and technologically advanced business enterprises—Ford, IBM, Exxon, etc.—that had arisen in the previous twenty years since the end of World War II. He revealed how technology, which he defined broadly as "the systematic application of scientific or other organized knowledge to practical tasks," had dramatically changed the economic landscape.

Since that book was published, a lot has changed, but the basic trends it identified have persisted. With the rise of Google, Facebook, and others, technology has expanded in ways Galbraith couldn't have dreamed. But a lot has also stayed the same—in particular, his observation that technology would be used to expand and maintain the wealth and power of the global elite.

In 2019, Tom and I engaged in a week of conversation to lay out the outline of this book and began writing it together. However, Tom's political life took hold and as his Foreign Affairs Committee and later security roles grew, he withdrew from the authoring. So I finished the book alone, although I tried to recognize both the differences and similarities between the US and the UK. Opinions, conclusions, and recommendations are mine alone.

Technology has remade our world in so many ways. While the direct effects are obvious and have been covered many times, it is the indirect effects which have left us so divided and unequal. Going forward, these effects are unlikely to lessen.

I hope this book helps to bring some clarity and understanding.

Bill Raduchel

INTRODUCTION

There were earlier efforts (notably by Charles Babbage), but modern computing—computers as we know them—sprang from the minds of Alan Turing and John Von Neumann at the Institute for Advanced Study at Princeton less than a hundred years ago.

Computers at first were seen as a curiosity, and at best as a scientific tool. They were certainly not seen as "personal."

Legend has it that the then-boss of IBM, Thomas J. Watson, estimated worldwide demand toward the end of World War II at five computers. This sounds ridiculous, of course, but it is only fair to remind ourselves that the machines of which he was thinking were vast, expensive congregations of vacuum tubes that took up an entire floor of a building, bearing very little resemblance to the featherweight machines that we throw into a pocket or onto a wrist today.

If Watson (who died in 1956) could see the marvel of a machine that I hold in my hands now (upon one of which this chapter is being written), he would be astounded, just as, no doubt, we will be by the next iteration of technological innovation—perhaps a nanocomputer small enough to be injected into the human body to perform biochemical procedures.

Even then, though huge and (from a modern perspective) primitive as they might have been, one could certainly argue that it was these new computers that truly won World War II. Without the intelligence gained from breaking German and Japanese codes, the war might easily have ended in a very different way.

Fifty years ago, we became focused on all the wonderful things technology could do for us—and technology has flowed like water ever since. Looking at our lives today, half a century later, the impact of his technology upon human existence defies estimation. Wartime code breaking, vital as it unquestionably was, constitutes merely the tip of what is today an immense iceberg.[1]

But this book is not really about technology. It is about power, efficiency, fragility, inequality, division, and economic rents, all of which are dramatically affected by technology. What this book is really about is society: about how it has changed and about what technology is enabling us to do to ourselves. Technology itself is neutral, of course. It can be used for good or evil. Sometimes, though, figuring out which is which can be difficult.

Writing *The New Industrial State* in 1967, the economist John Kenneth Galbraith was incredibly prescient. Although not a technologist himself, Galbraith did foresee something that others missed: the extraordinary power that technology has to transform society wholesale by altering the basic fabric of our lives. Galbraith warned then that the global elite would be sure to use technology to accumulate both wealth and power. Of course, he was right. In the half-century since he published the book, they have done precisely that.

In the late 1970s, the vector of technological change experienced a fundamental transformation. In Galbraith's time, technological change was driven by hardware. Although hardware continues to improve (driven by the continuous improvements in semi-conductors), innovation is increasingly driven by software. Artificial intelligence, for example, is just software. And software is a mysterious art to all but a select few. Software innovation can be incredibly fast and performed by a team as small as one individual.

Just as the rise of the multinational corporation defined the world John Kenneth Galbraith explored in *The New*

Industrial State, our epoch is defined by technology—technology so omnipresent it has become as fundamental as our DNA.

Today we are living in the New Technology State.

Too Efficient

Classical and neoclassical economics have unquestionably had a great run. For well over two centuries, the basic principles set out by Adam Smith and David Ricardo have dominated western thought. Against the bulwark of capitalism, communism and socialism have failed every test. And yet (as the modern writer Thomas Piketty has noted) the body of theory that constitutes neoclassical economics is fundamentally a theory of inequality. It accepts inequality precisely because we increase the degree to which society as a whole can prosper by permitting it. We grow the whole cake to such a degree that even the smallest slices are larger than they otherwise would have been: a more unequal world is also a more prosperous world for everyone. A rising tide lifts all boats.

The conventional wisdom is that governments can redistribute income to compensate for this inequality, always provided that the taxes they impose do not overly distort incentives—i.e., that they do not disrupt efficiency. However, as Galbraith taught, the conventional wisdom is almost always wrong.

Efficiency is the altar for classical economics. It is the holy grail. Pure economic efficiency entails all resources being optimally produced and then optimally distributed. Greater efficiency is always a good thing . . . at least in theory. Thus, to change the distribution of outcomes, one must accept lower overall output unless one can find a way to redistribute income without distorting incentives. This is a tough challenge and presents tough choices.

Neoclassical economics was born in an era of stagnation. Adam Smith published his great, foundational work *The Wealth of Nations* in 1776, when wealth was accruing on land but not on labor. His earlier book, *The Theory of Moral Sentiments*, spawns more subtle lines of inquiry, including one observation that bears repeating here: people want both to be loved and to be lovely. One may be wise to ask how technology has affected society's views on what it means to be lovely and how that in turn has affected the drive for efficiency.

During the final quarter of the eighteenth century and into the nineteenth, by contrast, there was massive and relatively rapid change. This change inevitably brought with it enormous social disruption. I was asked in graduate school to name the most critical technology to the Industrial Revolution. Students rushed, of course, to suggest the steam engine, the cotton gin, or the Bessemer converter. However, to the professor, the answer had to do with another kind of gin altogether. It was the gin still. It was this, the professor argued, which made substantial social change and upheaval possible. It was simply impossible to brew enough beer each day to provide the necessary amount of alcohol to get everyone who wanted to get drunk drunk! While the other inventions did, of course, help enormously, they had negative consequences—consequences that needed to be alleviated by the alcohol.

The upheaval effected by modern technological change is equally pronounced. And we still have gin stills and plenty of other drugs, legal and otherwise—smartphones and social media are as addictive as many "psychoactive" chemical compounds. This book is about these changes, the changes that are taking place now. It is not about the technological detail—constantly changing as it is—but rather about technology's impact on society more broadly: its impact on our lives and how the world around us will transform utterly as a result of it. Much of this change is undoubtedly very beneficial. But not all of it. This book will consider three negative longer-term effects of the contemporary upheaval.

Firstly, technology has made our economy too efficient, which necessarily reduces the robustness and resilience of markets. We have made ourselves fragile and our systems much more exposed to threats such as pandemic, war, or cybersecurity failure. Natural limits on the quality and availability of software talent make this inevitable. The drive for efficiency above all else has made our world much more complex, to the advantage of the few and the disadvantage of the many.

Secondly, and on that note, the vast economic "rents" have driven inequality to what many argue are socially damaging levels. To Ricardo, rents were incomes above what one could earn through labor, or incomes gleaned from scarcity. He was mainly focused on land. Ricardo had a simple solution for rents: tax them all away. The scarce assets today are often intangible, but that does not invalidate the point.

And thirdly, society is now so fractured—so deeply divided—that we now disagree perpetually, and we barely interact with those in other camps. The profound fissures within the political life of the US and the UK and other nations illustrate this all too clearly. This is an ugly part of human nature, but technology has optimized the ability to leverage this ugliness by empowering narratives over facts. It may indeed have changed ugliness into the new meaning of lovely.

THE AGE OF
THE ALGORITHM

Farmers, politicians, and economists are constantly struggling to predict the future. Will the sunrise be a warning or a comfort? Will the data show a good crop or a strong economy? Will the polls give reassurance that the people agree?

At each turn, inputs are collected and evaluated. They are tuned and polished to provide the best chance of an accurate reading and, just when the model shows a confident output, the world steps in with a surprise. The trouble with real life is that it's so unpredictable.

This isn't new. Humans have been trying to run programs that turn data into divination for thousands of years. Those who have achieved it—by luck or skill—have been rewarded by society.

The earliest attempts were probably connected to the appeasement of the gods to encourage a good hunt or harvest. Actions meant to bring rain or fertility were likely built on the memory that earlier efforts had succeeded. Those actions were now structured procedures for success. Later attempts saw mystics reading the entrails of sacrificial animals to understand the plan of the gods for the outcome of wars.

In Egypt, Greece, Mexico, India, Persia, and many other places around the world scientists built (often amazingly good) instruments of stone, wood, iron, and gold to chart the heavens—not just out of curiosity, but because the movements of the planets foretold the destiny of kings. They invented new ways of counting the passage of time and distance to foretell the appearance of comets. Their techniques informed the sciences and shaped our world, even if the core of their beliefs was no more than a dream.

One of the greatest exponents of the forecasting science emerged in the ninth century where the Oxus River begins. In a now long-forgotten town in Turkmenistan, a Persian mathematician, astrologer, and scientist was born. Abu Abdallah Mohammed bin Musa al-Khwarizmi (or, in English: Father of Abdallah, Mohammed, son of Moses, from Khwarizm) developed advanced mathematics to calculate the movements of the stars.

Moving to the increasingly powerful capital of Baghdad under the Abbasid dynasty, al-Khwarizmi became the astronomer to the House of Wisdom, as the great library was called. During his time there he studied maps and charts, geography and trigonometry, and created equations to measure distance and calculate movement. Taken together, this created algebra, or "the balancing," named after his book *The Compendious Book on Calculation by Completion and Balancing.*

Al-Khwarizmi's science required mathematical operations impossible with the Roman numerals still prevalent in the West. Around 820, al-Khwarizmi's work *On the Calculation with Hindu Numerals* spread the Arabic numerals we use today around Europe. Originating in India, these numerals allowed for equations and calculations that would otherwise be impossible. Such was the importance of his work that when Europe woke up to the science of the Islamic world around the eleventh century, al-Khwarizmi was translated into Latin and his name was attached to the equations themselves as *algoritmi*. His work, and his name, created a branch of mathematics that was built not only on the ability to calculate movement but on the idea that science could predict the future.

Today, algorithms continue to be used to predict the

future, but the data available is so vast that the equations can go further than even al-Khwarizmi could have imagined. The building blocks of our bodies—the proteins that shape our very beings—can now be used to predict our personal futures. The detail available has turned digital priests into prophets and given extraordinary power to the software engineers who write the code—the new shamans who brew the algorithms that determine our lives.

Whenever we say "the computer did it," what we mean is that some algorithm running on some computer made a decision. But it was never a computer, or rather never a computer alone. A person, writing software, created a series of commands based on inputs to determine a future. One important thing has changed with this level of complexity—instead of interpreting the natural order, these codes alter it. They read so much that isn't written, and interpret so much more than anyone could know, that they conjure up outcomes that were once unimaginable.

Computer algorithms are everywhere today. Algorithms determine whether or not we get a job or a loan. They determine the airline fare we pay and whether our absentee ballot is accepted. They decide what information we read on a website or social media platform, as well as who gets seen first in a hospital and what treatment they receive. The list is endless.

The illusion they offer is omniscience, but algorithms are not perfect—though, by design, they assume that they are. They are created by humans to achieve a purpose, and they rely on assumptions about the minutiae of data we create as we go about our lives. This opens the world to the multiplication of error. From input to assumption, simple mistakes (accidental or deliberate) can change outcomes as surely as the authors of chaos theory predicted storms. This time, the beating of the butterfly's wings doesn't just cause storms, it changes lives.

An objective may be too narrow and doesn't account for enough variability. Assumptions may be based on limited understanding or inadequate forethought. There will be unintended consequences, both good and bad. Perhaps most important, however, is the illusion of precision. In reality, results may not only be vague, they may be trying to answer the wrong question altogether.

Smaller, Faster, Cheaper

Galbraith had it right when he wrote that the global elite would use technology to accumulate wealth and power. The mechanism for that accumulation has been the algorithm, propelled by ever cheaper, more powerful computers accessing ever more and more detailed data. Perhaps this is the Age of the Algorithm. Today, we hear more and more about artificial intelligence and machine learning, but both of these are all about algorithms—algorithms so good they mimic human thought (artificial intelligence) and algorithms created by other algorithms parsing through mounds of data (machine learning).

The result has been an accumulation of magnified, multiplied change over the last two decades. Smaller, faster, cheaper computers enable ever more powerful algorithms, expanding their uses and impact. These algorithms have divided our society, and they have made money doing it. As algorithms became more valuable, the people who could create and tune them also became more valuable, and teams of them even more so. Those who could attract and retain them became the dominant organizations in the world, the new churches of a new religion.

Algorithms have also changed the way we organize ourselves. We have gone beyond collective farming and beyond planting and harvesting according to the advice of those who could read the weather, all the way to the enterprise resource planning of the 1990s that made businesses more efficient but less robust. We have minimized doubt and underprepared for alternative outcomes, leading to leaner, more efficient systems—and to a level of risk few could have predicted but which the recent pandemic has exposed. The next turn of this screw will bring us DAOs, distributed autonomous organizations: your actual boss will be an algorithm.

Algorithms now shape how nations defend themselves and attack others. Cyberwar is no longer science fiction. An August 2020 experiment by the US showed that AI could routinely out-fly, out-think, and, of course, shoot down the best human pilot, largely because the AI could fly at the limit of the plane rather than that of the human. It seems obvious when you hear it, but the revelation was transformational. Instead of megatons, the future of warfare will hinge on chip nanometers.

With all these changes, the structures that have kept society together are under intense pressure. Community cohesion is challenged, and even the future of the nation-state is no longer assured.

For decades, philosophers and science fiction writers have worried about an inevitable battle between technology and humans. When will technology be smart enough to try to take over? The movie *2001: A Space Odyssey* brought this home to the masses. Elon Musk has argued that the victory of the machine is inevitable because machines will have greater and faster access to data than humans, even if human processing ability is superior. He has funded the company Neuralink to improve the ability of the human brain to process external data.

Most discussion about the viability of cryptocurrency misses a far more significant point: blockchain technologies and cryptocurrencies create the ability for algorithms to be self-actuating—they can both accept and disperse money.

This is profound. Until this, algorithms could only instruct humans. Now they can conduct commerce without them. But an even more critical change engendered by the invention of blockchain is the creation of digital scarcity.

Digitization was always about infinite copying. Now we have digital assets that are limited. Combine that with the fact that software now has the ability to pay a human or be paid by a human without human intervention—and cryptocurrencies become essentially a hedge against government breakdown.

In the long run, if nation-states are no longer the bedrock, cryptoassets are inevitable.

Eating the World

The way to conquer the mind is not to capture it but to mislead it. Propaganda is undoubtedly almost as old as humankind, but Joseph Goebbels used it to enormous effect to empower the Nazis in Germany and made one thing horrifyingly clear: we—humans—are susceptible to manipulation. We hate mistakes more than we enjoy making the right decision. We respond to emotion many times more than we respond to reason. We make voting decisions on no more than three factors. As we age, we trust our instincts more and require more data to change our beliefs. We trust even casual acquaintances more than distant experts. Our imaginations can mislead our bodies, as even the success of the pornography industry shows.

Thus, we are fertile ground for algorithms. No one foresaw what we were about to do to ourselves as we rolled out successive rounds of innovation. We celebrated each new advance. The global internet. Smartphones with a camera and GPS. App stores. Social media. Anything seemed possible. Online services with a billion users. Now four billion. All amazing. Personalized information. Personalized entertainment. Personalized news. What could go wrong?

These new services were wonderful, and they were also enormously profitable. We were said to be in the Attention

Economy. Gaining your attention became the pathway to riches, and algorithms provided the way to secure them. In truth, we are in the Algorithm Economy.

A harbinger of what was to come came in the 1990s, when corporations migrated to enterprise resource planning (ERP) systems. ERP systems allow algorithms to run businesses. Costs went down. Cash flows improved. Time and place mattered less. Algorithms significantly reduced the cost of global transit because containerization is not possible without computer algorithms to track and bill. In short, algorithms made globalization and outsourcing possible—and made taxes easily transferable between countries. Companies were free to locate operations wherever was best economically. Globalization went unchecked until tensions between the US and China (and then Covid-19) put on the brakes. As of this writing, the conflict in Ukraine continues to challenge the system as it stands.

Importantly, algorithms have made much labor increasingly less meaningful. Humans are peripheral to systems ruled by algorithms. The skills pyramid became less like a pyramid in shape and more like a volcano—a volcano that may be on the verge of eruption.

The people who understood how to exploit algorithms became both wealthy and powerful. Marc Andreessen famously said "software is eating the world," but the reality was that the software was implementing algorithms. Those with the necessary skills to create, enhance, and operate them turned out to be incredibly scarce. They are not evil. They just seek out the best opportunity for themselves in the market economy in which we live, and those who create, sell, and use algorithms can both pay the most and provide the most meaningful work. This is nothing new. Arms merchants with new technology have always been able to extract wealth and power from those needing their wares. The Vikings conquered their world with 1,000 steel swords. These top developers are the modern-day equivalent.

Computer scientists love AB testing. The concept is simple: if you have an interaction between a human and a system, try it two different ways and choose the one that works best. This is deep in the DNA of anyone who is good at building these systems. Google runs thousands of these tests every day. Algorithms run these AB tests and pick (or even write) the best story headline. They learn which stories you are most likely to click. AB testing is inherently neutral, but its results are strongly biased by human weakness. The results are all around us. Hate is much more profitable than reason; hatred in a political context, emotion generally, and of course sex. The result is that we divide and inflame in the pursuit of attention and profit.

However, there is an even more significant issue with algorithms. Algorithms brilliantly automate the tasks best accomplished by the left side of the human brain. But the left side of our brains is only half the story. Empathy, creativity, nuance—these are the province of our right hemispheres, which we do not know how to model well.

So the world of algorithms is a world devoted to efficiency but devoid of compassion. Should we be surprised that we are where we are?

FACEBOOK'S ANGRY INVISIBLE HAND

Two decades ago, AOL defined the consumer internet, and people commented on all the great things you could do with it. The reality, however, is that what people did on it was communicate in email, instant messaging, message boards, and chat rooms. Communication was so dominant that Steve Case, its CEO, thought that AOL's future was as a communications company and joined the board of directors of a telecom to learn more.

When Mark Zuckerberg and others created Facebook at Harvard in 2004, it seemed like a niche product. Indeed, the rollout was methodical and slow, but Zuckerberg's ambitions were the opposite. Facebook has long since surpassed anything AOL ever dreamed of.

Still, AOL left Facebook an incredible legacy in the US

Communications Decency Act and its most famous provision, Section 230. As you read that section, you need to be thinking AOL chat rooms, not Facebook news feed. No one even dreamed that something like a news feed was feasible when that law was written. Today, TikTok has taken the news feed concept to an entirely new level.

What 230 did was say that the service provider was not accountable for what someone else said on its service, as long as the service moderated the content. If someone misbehaved in a chat room, AOL could not be sued or charged. How AOL beat its well-heeled competitor Prodigy was by allowing more topics in chat rooms (AOL let teenagers talk about sex; Prodigy did not). The public chat rooms were monitored though, and AOL had an army of volunteer moderators who watched the chats. Unlike today, these were volunteers whose only compensation was free service, though there was a paid staff as well. In part because the volunteers could not be tightly managed, the other portion of Section 230 said that AOL or any other provider could not be sued or charged by a reasonable act of moderation.

Zuckerberg invented what today dominates Facebook and almost every other social media platform: the feed. You get presented with a never-ending list of posts and sponsored items selected to engage you. The news feed has evolved to be something different than the AOL chat room. If you have ever worked in a newspaper or a magazine or produced a video, you understand one fundamental truth: high quality requires lots of content to be thrown away. The ratio varies with quality, but you need three to ten times as much content to choose from as you have room to publish. Often, the rest is left on the cutting room floor.

From its billions of users, Facebook has a wealth of content from which to choose. In the beginning, the brilliance of Adam D'Angelo, the first CTO at Facebook, was to front-end their storage with lots and lots of Memcached servers to maximize the amount of available content. He was very successful, but that then created a new problem: How to choose?

The answer to that is an algorithm. Algorithms only need an objective function: something to maximize. User satisfaction would be an obvious choice, but how do you define that? As anyone who has watched *The Social Dilemma* on Netflix can tell you, the algorithm maximizes click-throughs, which is not a terrible proxy for satisfaction. It certainly has not hurt Facebook's revenue and profits. Mind you, these algorithms are built out of machine learning. Algorithms are amoral. They have no soul.

Told to maximize clicks, they will maximize clicks in the most efficient way possible.

Unfortunately, anger boosts the likelihood that you will click through. Humans are humans, and emotion matters. Thus, an unemotional algorithm will quickly evolve to understand that success comes from making you angry and emotional. Balance and reason are not favored by such an algorithm. No one is doing anything wrong here. This is just like the Microsoft Twitter bot Tay that quickly learned to be racist.[1]

Under the law, what exactly is an algorithm—especially a sophisticated algorithm like that used by Facebook to order its news feed? In other venues, the big tech companies are arguing that what algorithms produce is protected by copyright, which means by default that the algorithm is an author.

This is profound, because authors are responsible for what they create. Section 230 does not protect them. Recently, Justice Clarence Thomas questioned in an official Supreme Court publication whether the courts had gone too far in extending the protections afforded by Section 230. A legislative or judicial declaration that provider-programmed algorithms are authors would resolve many issues—and create many as well.

The consequences of algorithmic behavior are not trivial. Facebook created the news feed on its way to amassing more than four billion users. As a profit-maximizing company, Facebook maximized user engagement. Humans being humans respond more to anger than reason. As Facebook grew and grew, its users became more and more polarized. People in many countries trust Facebook as their principal source of news. Hence, we end up with nations divided.

Algorithms also changed the economics of media, and Facebook was among the first to recognize and exploit this. There used to be an economic constraint on extreme views. You needed advertising to support the media, and advertising required signing up advertisers. To do that you needed a sales force and an ad-delivery operation. This limited the number of effective competitors to a few, which in turn meant they all had to appeal to the middle of the market; Walter Cronkite, the legendary TV news anchor, was as much a creature of economics as of journalism. A website or a channel or a show or a publication with marginal views and viewers had difficulty finding advertising dollars to support it.

That all changed with Facebook. First, no matter how extreme the views on a particular feed, to an advertiser it was simply a Facebook impression, and all Facebook ads were seen as "brand safe." Second, no one had more personal data on the owner of the eyeballs viewing the ad than Facebook, so the ability of Facebook to target ads was unmatched. Extremism paid Facebook. No evil intent necessary. These are just the unintended consequences of seemingly good business decisions driven only by revenue and profit.

The power of Facebook became clear in the 2016 US presidential election, in which Donald Trump spent $150 million on targeted ads in the last three weeks of the campaign in five counties, four of which provided the 78,000-vote margin that elected him president. He did his own targeting on his own data and used the power of Facebook to buy ads by name. Politicians worldwide took note. Never before had a candidate run ads to discourage voting, which he did to great effect, helped by the fact that he did not have to disclose his sponsorship.

Similar changes have happened elsewhere on the internet, where today over a trillion times a day auctions are held to determine which ad is shown to the viewer. This takes massive but cheap computer power, fast networks, and lots of data. Much of the time the ad slot may go to remnant ads that are untargeted and pay little, but they can be an order of magnitude more valuable. Most ad targeting has to be done in less than one fifth of a second, which was unfeasible until recently, so this is a recent phenomenon.

To make this a perfect storm for Facebook, one more thing was required: the mobile internet. If you had to dial up on a personal computer sitting at a desk, none of this would have mattered as much. However, with the enormous proliferation of the smartphone and ever cheaper data services, the phone became nearly ubiquitous worldwide and Facebook became constantly available. Indeed, in the run-up to its initial public offering, Facebook struck deals worldwide for zero rating as a marketing tool for carriers, which meant using Facebook was free but using anything else was charged against their data allowance. It worked. Brilliant.

Facebook expanded its reach even more by offering Facebook Connect, which let consumers log into other sites using their Facebook credentials. The site got data from Facebook, while Facebook in turn gained even more knowledge about its users. Similarly, Facebook encouraged firms to use Pages on Facebook instead of a standalone site, again offering data in return. When someone liked a site, they unknowingly shared data with it. It may be true that Facebook never sold its users' data, but they certainly traded it for commercial gain.

Again, Facebook did all this as though guided by an invisible hand. Not for nefarious purposes. Just maximizing its profits and return to shareholders. Unfortunately, this story does not end here. The returns to the shareholders have been great, but they pale compared to the negative external consequences.

Chris Hughes is a smart, charismatic, charming young man. He was Zuckerberg's roommate at Harvard and headed marketing for Facebook when it was a nascent blip on the horizon. He left Facebook early to take over social media for the first presidential campaign for Barack Obama, and he succeeded beyond any measure in raising campaign money from small donors. This was hailed at the time for reducing reliance on major donors. Politicians everywhere have built on this success ever since. Today fundraising by email, text message, and social media is the name of the game for political fundraising.

But if we read any portion of these electronic appeals for donation, we can see immediately that raising money this way is not any different from the core of the attention economy: emotion trumps all. Extreme views raise more money than balanced views. Everyone is captive to his or her base, and raising money from the base is best accomplished through fear. This is human nature, and it is not subject to easy regulation. As long as donations drive politics, there will be a strong bias in political discourse to extremes, amplifications, and divisions.

Politics was once seen as a noble profession, a way to give back. That seems quaint today. Candidates today face intense scrutiny of their personal lives going back routinely to their teenage years. Compensation is far below market levels in almost all countries but Singapore. Where there is no public funding for campaigns, the real job is fundraising, and policymaking is a sideline.

Being a politician today takes commitment, and all too often that commitment comes from extreme views. Less than twenty years ago, such candidates would have had difficulty fundraising. Not today.

DATA IS THE NEW OIL

Data is the new oil. This is not a new observation, nor is it totally correct. However, like petroleum, data is not produced by those who pump it, and it should be taxed as is oil from the ground. We need to treat aggregated personally identifiable information as a public good and tax its use. We can debate the level, but it should not be zero. We also need to understand that data is a weapon. Russia, China, North Korea, and Iran all understand this. Data allows them to cybermeddle in our societies to drive division and unrest.

Also like petroleum, data must be refined to be valuable. Until the present, the costs of doing so have been prohibitive for all but a few special cases. Today, artificial intelligence and machine learning and cloud computing have made these refining costs almost negligible, so that we can cost-effectively apply them to placing a single online advertisement—a trillion times a day. Any business is at root an information system, and so any business could be transformed by that kind of processing—airlines started it by creating virtual goods, leading to multiple prices for the same seat.

Creating and operating software requires significant skill and lore. Like the talent that creates it, organizations that can manage and exploit it are incredibly advantaged. Witness Amazon: even when software talent is highly paid, the productivity of a team of exceptionally talented software engineers is even greater, so that firms can pay the workers above market but below value. This drives the creation of technology giants. Traditional antitrust doctrine fits into this scheme poorly, if at all. The more talent you aggregate, the more productive and profitable you become. Just as the Middle East has played a disproportionate role in the world because of its control of oil, so the technology giants are playing a disproportionate role because of their control of both data and talent. When countries are designating "ambassadors" to Google, the world has changed.

Just as with petroleum, inequality has been an inevitable result. Control of talent and data leads to wealth. Technology removes requisite skills from jobs, enabling a broader labor pool to compete for them and thereby lowering the compensation. At the same time, it makes those at the top of the pyramid—those producing and funding that technology—more valuable. To the extent that this is based on scarcity, Ricardo would argue that much of this compensation qualifies as rents, which should therefore be taxed away.

These trends have been amplified by tax code provisions providing highly favorable treatment to stock-based compensation as long as stock prices increase. Employees have been able to earn significant compensation while their companies gain massive tax savings from a non-cash expense. In the US, the managers of hedge funds and private equity firms (including venture capital) are able to get capital gains treatment on their carried interest, which is the bulk of their compensation. Efforts to end that practice always seem to fail because the beneficiaries of that break provide enormous political funding.

Technology and media have a long, intertwined history, with copyright law often serving as a battleground. Consumers want personalized entertainment. If you doubt this, look at children on their tablets. Consumers see no moral issue in "sharing" content, but content owners want to be paid. In the end, personalized entertainment wins.

The president of the Korean Broadcast System has explained the importance of the high-production-value content they produce with the help of government subsidies. The government believed it was the glue that helped hold Korean society and values together. Korean TV shows are simply better than a country that size might ordinarily produce, and they are watched all over Asia as a result. But they have helped to mold a foundation of values. In the 1950s and 1960s, the three principal network shows and advertisements did the same in the US, as did the BBC in the UK. That is lost with personalized entertainment.

Technology now allows consumers to get the personalized entertainment they want and allows content owners to get paid, though many ambiguous areas remain. The advertising ecosystem mentioned above now allows advertising to be personalized as well, so that the need for direct advertising sales has evaporated. There is no longer a huge scale advantage: any audience platform can earn economic returns.

In this algorithm economy, the barrier to success and the major cost is the acquisition and retention of eyeballs. Starting with Rupert Murdoch's Fox News, audience platforms have discovered that telling viewers what they already believe is the winning strategy. Aggregating the largest audience is not as important as aggregating the most loyal. By this calculation, moderation is the enemy. Amplification, not attenuation, is the order of the day. This needs to be repeated: the attention economy rewards amplification, not attenuation. Again, watch *The Social Dilemma*.

Or look at *Bad News* by Batya Ungar-Sargon. Her basic thesis is that the dependence of the major news sites on their relatively small population of subscribers has inevitably turned them into echo chambers where the journalists and the subscribers all come from the same class of affluent, highly educated elites. Algorithms drive all this, with the Murdoch effect enforcing alignment and journalists being rewarded for their conformed content, which in turn drives subscriptions and brings in data.

A further consequence of this data-driven technology has been the increased rate of social discount, the rate at which the current generations discount the welfare of future generations in making decisions. Technology makes immediate concentrated pain much more real and makes diffuse future benefits seem much more abstract. This is one reason the inherent long-term risks of climate change so often fall on deaf ears.

As discussed above, the 2016 presidential election in the United States showed the power of this scheme. Clinton spent most of her funds on television ads attacking Trump's character. Trump spent $150 million in FIVE counties (there are over 3,000) in the last three weeks of the campaign, using a new feature of Facebook that let advertisers target ads by individual name. Trump (or rather Brad Parscale) spent half that money encouraging people not to vote. The other half went to encouraging known supporters to show up. Trump carried Wisconsin, Michigan, and Pennsylvania as a result. In the UK, it was reported that the Labour Party used this same feature to run ads its leader wanted—but only to him.

The true geniuses who created the internet never dreamed of its current scale. They envisioned a million users who could be trusted to be responsible. We are far from that today. *The Perfect Weapon* on HBO lays bare the risks we now face; they are as cataclysmic as the atomic weapons of 1945.

The reactions of government so far are not surprising. If you do not know the story of US general Billy Mitchell, go read it. A hero of World War I, Mitchell was court-martialed in the 1920s for saying battleships were outmoded and could be sunk by airplanes—and then proving it. The US Army recently decided to drop basic training for cyber command recruits. The US Marine Corps just announced a new talent strategy in which talent that is not going into physical combat will no longer do basic training, and talent with experience can enter at an appropriate rank.

What is the future of the nation-state in all this? Facebook has nearly three times as many users as the Catholic Church has adherents. Data flows seamlessly, anywhere, instantly. The military has long understood that people do not fight for king and country but for their buddies. Electronic allegiance to friends and family is replacing allegiance to country, society, and (for many) religion. Dating apps alone are multibillion dollar businesses. Data is the new oil.

HALSTEAD LENGTH

Throughout human history, people have understood that, in terms of abilities or skills—both mental and physical—not all members of our species are the same, any more than we are the same in terms of our tastes for food, or drink, or love, or sexual gratification, our preferences for literature, for music, for art, or for physical activity. Software talent is today akin to that of star athletes or entertainers, and equally scarce.

Society comprises many different people, with a wide variety of strengths and passions. The structure of the brain is only beginning to be understood, and a vast amount still remains mysterious. But we are starting to make some headway as computing technology and artificial intelligence accelerate, even if what we learn only reinforces our astonishment, and admiration, for what millions of years of evolution have achieved (obliging agreement with the economist John Kay's comment that a better synopsis of evolution than "survival of the fittest" would be "evolution is smarter than you").[1]

In terms of human intelligence, it is obviously true that only a tiny number of us have the capacity to be a Go grandmaster, regardless of our understanding of, or practice at, the game. The great majority of us could dedicate as much time as we liked to the pursuit without ever becoming anywhere near good enough. The same thing is more widely true: it has become increasingly clear that it is only a tiny number of very unusual people, possessed of very unusual capacities or skills, who are disproportionately able to advance humanity's understanding of the world and to advance its technological capabilities—or to develop, maintain, and improve complex computer algorithms. Those who do, the Canadian economist Reuven Brenner referred to as the Vital Few, and this is certainly what they are: perhaps only half of 1 percent of the total population qualifies, and sometimes a good deal less than that.[2]

It simply isn't the case that anyone who spends 10,000 hours practicing a given activity in youth will reach an elite standard. Yes, Roger Federer has practiced tennis a lot. But he is certainly not the only one to have done so. Across a wide array of countries, you can attend junior tennis tournaments and observe a very high level of competitiveness and desire on display (amongst both players and watching parents) in the certain knowledge that most if not all of these players will not progress anywhere near the lucrative upper echelons of the sport. More than time on the court separates Roger Federer from almost all other tennis players. As the great majority who have played competitive sports well know, the playing field is simply not level.

Let us look now at mental agility or intelligence. We have only begun to comprehend the workings of the human brain, but our current understanding of IQ is that there are four principal measures, three of which do not diverge that widely between humans and so cannot possibly account for the wide range of intelligence with which we are familiar. The one-time professional cricketer Ed Smith makes precisely this point with reference to cricket in his book *Luck*, where he points out that the enormous talent of his contemporary, Kevin Pietersen, could simply not be explained with reference to practice alone.

American psychologist John M. Stroud may have been the first to estimate the brain's processing rate. The article in which Stroud made this estimate was published in the late 1960s under the title "The Fine Structure of Psychological Time." Using some impressively accurate guesstimating, Stroud calculated the time taken by the human brain to perform an elementary discrimination and concluded that this varied within the human population by a ratio of perhaps 4:1—a figure very close to the 3:1 difference reported by modern researchers. What he was calculating here was *speed* of thought, not *depth* of thought. (While some work might require one to think quickly, perhaps literally on one's feet, it is perfectly possible to be rapid and flashy but not profound, and perfectly possible too to be a brilliant, but slow, thinker.)[3]

Brain Train

To explain the variance in brain performance requires more, however, so we need to look at human memory, which appears to be structured in discrete chunks, or containers, of information. When a chunk is open, all of its contents are instantly available to the person concerned. It seems that humans average around seven chunks open at any one time. This number does vary between individual human beings, but, again, the range of variation is quite narrow, between around twelve chunks open and around three: a similar ratio, therefore, of 4:1.

Beyond these are what might be called *thought generators*, responsible for the production of original thoughts, which are subsequently evaluated. Since these are simply random perturbations of our past experience as preserved by our brains, it follows that the richer and more diverse are our pasts, the better and more original will be our thoughts or innovations. This of course is why we hire consultants: it is not that they are seeing fundamentally different information than the employees of a firm, it is that they are able to detect in it patterns and interactions that may be invisible to those without the same breadth of experience.

In the same way, significant originality in thought—or in poetical language, for example—may be created by the ability to draw parallels between what seem at first glance to be unrelated fields of experience. The subsequent process of evaluation—in which a decision is made as to whether the thoughts are valuable ones, worth preserving—is not one we yet understand, though the brain is quickly able to perform pattern recognition on them and to reject random or unappealing thoughts until it finds one that it likes.

Using brain scans, it is possible to count how many such thought generators a person has at his or her disposal. Again, the range is actually quite narrow: between around two and ten, with an average of around five. Even if the variation is a little larger, in other words—perhaps 5:1—it remains very small, and certainly does not account for the wide discrepancy in intelligence among humans.

What does vary a lot, however, is the fourth measure of mental capacity. This concerns the size of a memory chunk: how much information, in other words, one chunk is capable of containing. It is this that the late Maurice Halstead (an early computer programmer and author of the 1977 work *Elements of Software Science*) referred to as Halstead Length.[6] While the average amount of information contained in one of these chunks might be 250 (an arbitrary metric, equating to 50 lines of the software written in the Fortran language) a very wide degree of variation among humans makes it perfectly possible for the highest scores to be over 60,000—more than 240 times the average.

Now, the longer one's Halstead Length, the more complex the problem one is capable of understanding. But it isn't simply a question of length. It is a question too of the way in which this information is stored: of what computer scientists call data structure. Obviously, for very small amounts of information storage is not complex. As the volume of information becomes much larger, however, the data structure in which it is stored is able to become much richer and more sophisticated.

Since it is the links between information that are all-important—because they crucially shape the ease of access and the connections the brain makes between different parts of it—the data itself becomes not only more voluminous but also more meaningful according to how it is stored. If you then multiply the contents of a chunk (bearing in mind the elaborate links and structure preserved within it) by the number of chunks accessible at any one time, you get a variation between humans that approaches 1,000:1—a very significant difference that does match the diverse intelligence we see in an Albert Einstein on the one hand and someone of low IQ on the other.

A few pictures will help explain precisely why it is that this makes such a large difference. The picture on the next page is of a familiar scene, containing a huge amount of information by way of detail. Suppose that this image represents the problem one hopes to solve, the challenge being to understand the entire image:

Assume that you are a person with a capacity for seven chunks, each of Halstead Length 250. What you can understand of this image at one time looks like this:

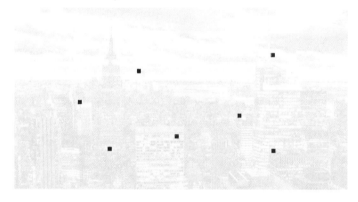

Obviously, this is not very interesting or, indeed, very helpful. By repeatedly passing over the entire image, you may (with time) be able to gain a fuller understanding, but the work is tedious at best. Assume, however, that you are blessed with the ability to have seven simultaneous chunks of Halstead Length 65,000. Now what you see looks like this:

Obviously, you still cannot see the whole picture, though if the problem were a bit smaller you could (and of course a team of two or three such people can see it all). Nevertheless, these chunks contain vastly more information and are a great deal more intelligible and manageable, while broad patterns and interactions between them are much more apparent. Furthermore, some people have more than seven chunks; and this example does not even allow for the greatly accentuated complexity of structure that has now become possible within each chunk.

Now imagine you adopt another approach. You reduce the level of detail of the overall image in order to make the broad patterns and interactions more visible to a person with seven chunks and a Halstead Length of 250. It allows them to see the whole image as opposed to only a tiny fraction of it—but it looks like this:

. . . which of course tells the viewer very little indeed about the content of the picture.

Now, what is interesting more broadly is that those who return a notably high score for their Halstead Length include not only computer programmers but also great artists, novelists, and musicians. Indeed, exceptional people in all spheres.

Imagine the brainpower required to conceive (never mind to execute) something like the structure of the Sistine Chapel ceiling, a large and complex literary work like *À la recherche du temps perdu*, or a long orchestral symphony containing multiple parts. This implies that these skills are often transferable, provided of course that the retraining is done at a sufficiently early age. A great musician may quite possibly be retrained to be a great computer programmer; the necessary brainpower is already there.

This point about early training is fundamental, because the brain of someone under the age of twenty is malleable in a way that the brain of someone older simply is not. "Give me a boy at seven," said Jesuit founder Ignatius of Loyola, "and I'll give you a Catholic for life." It is a sentiment with which modern science rather tends to agree—though it may also be the case that the brains of very small children are too malleable; formal education does not begin until the age of seven in a number of successful countries. One leading programmer, Alex St. John, found precisely the same thing while training people in their late teens to learn to be productive programmers in New Zealand. It even seems possible that a quality like Halstead Length can actually be improved, provided that you train early enough.

Brain Drain

The tech giants (Amazon, Google, Apple, Meta, and Microsoft) are well aware of the special and highly lucrative nature of their talent. They are anxious to retain their services and, in consequence, provide high compensation, primarily through stock options and stock grants. Individual developers at these companies can earn millions of dollars per year. The situation is no different to Paris Saint-Germain football club with regard to Lionel Messi, where the club's income depends upon his talents.

It is important again to note that there is nothing nefarious here in intent. These engineers are worth what they are paid. They like to work with other talented engineers, and they are incredibly productive in such teams. These companies have mastered all the cultural and ancillary tactics to make them both happy and productive. At most companies, being assigned to work on internal tools is seen as inferior; at Google it is an honor. That speaks volumes.

As the financial rewards for this ability have multiplied, the inequality has become more obvious. One particular skill (the ability to program) unquestionably enjoys an extreme financial benefit over many others. Most people who are very good at art, very good at theoretical mathematics, or very good at all sorts of other things, are simply not financially rewarded to anything like the same extent.

One of the consequences of this shift is a reduced emphasis upon an individual's education and experience—upon the classic entries on a CV concerning a person's school or university, the subjects and grades that they acquired there, or upon their previous places of work (much of which information was as much about establishing that a candidate knew the right people). What has happened is the replacement of this emphasis upon education and experience by emphasis purely upon skills and ability. For the firms in Silicon Valley, the only thing that truly matters is the ability to do the job.

This is much more true than it used to be, now that advanced computer literacy is rare and hard to acquire (though basic computer literacy is common); the pool of individuals who genuinely understand a complex area like AI, blockchain, or robotics is extremely small, even amongst those who otherwise are technologically literate. Google has just announced that, for employment purposes, it would consider the completion of some of its training programs to be the equivalent of a university degree.

So a few tens of thousands of people are highly paid. Why does that matter? Alone they do not materially change the Gini coefficient, the standard measure of income inequality. Any firm, any business, is a distributed information system with processors and networks, some of which are human and some technology. The links are becoming ever more sophisticated and the technology nodes more abundant. This small group of talent is the key to making that happen. A modern firm must be imagined as an inverted pyramid with its technologists at the bottom. Having great technology talent enables everything else.

The current conventional wisdom in Silicon Valley is that market compensation for a top software engineer with a year of experience is roughly $5 million over four years, most of which is paid in equity. The money gets paid only if the company achieves its projections, of course, but it does distort the labor market. Besides the technology giants and nascent unicorn startups, there are few companies that could ever match this compensation expectation. The rich will get richer and the poor poorer.

Industry lore says that twenty years ago Amazon decided that their core competency was creating and operating complex computer systems. Regardless, that is what Amazon is. They ring the cash register in many ways, but they really are a computer systems company. The same lore says Google made a similar but slightly different decision: they decided their core competency was in attracting, retaining, and managing great talent. Like Amazon, that is what they do.

Apple is quite different. They are still the cultural heirs of Steve Jobs, and Tim Cook has been a master at maintaining and milking that culture. Steve left them with a brilliant business model brilliantly implemented. The core competency of Apple today is software, something Steve learned from Avie Tevanian at NeXT (Avie created OSX, which remains the foundation of all Apple products today). Steve figured out how to bundle that software with hardware to maximize the value capture by Apple. In doing so he was following a model set by Sun Microsystems, which came within a signature of acquiring Apple in 1993. Everyone still envies that business model, but few have succeeded in copying it.

Meta is slightly different, still very much driven by its founder. It is an engineering culture with an incredibly profitable business model. It has all the engineering attractions of Google, but a more results-driven culture.

Like Amazon and Google, Meta is really a software company that develops and operates complex computer systems at a gigantic scale. To attract the talent they need, they have even contributed technology to open source licenses, which illuminates how hard this competition for talent really is. They have now begun an uncertain journey to reinvent themselves into the future based on the concept of a metaverse.

Finally there is Microsoft, which was once the industry bully but has now become more like the reawakened giant. They knew the talent game decades ago and bragged that in the mid-1990s they had more than half of the top 10,000 software developers then in the world on their payroll. Antitrust litigation slowed them down and made lawyers more important. The next few years will be interesting in that regard with respect to the other four.

Every business competes in the same labor market for this technology talent. Again, these are not marginal differences in output. The very top developers are sometimes two orders of magnitude better than the average. Teams of them may be three orders of magnitude better. The basic economics of software have not changed in the fifty years since Fred Brooks first wrote his *The Mythical Man-Month* about the creation of the operating system for IBM mainframes.

The big five US tech giants plus Tencent and a few others in China have captured the vast bulk of the available talent. Not by force. Not by doing anything illegal. Just by being good at recruiting and retaining them. But their skills and abilities allow their employees to earn massive economic returns. Other firms face an incredible challenge in securing the core competitive capability they need. This further drives inequality.

There is a recurring issue for which there seems no immediate answer. The distribution of these skills and abilities (of very high Halstead Lengths) is uneven, as you would expect for any such trait. White and Asian males dominate the current pool. There are exceptions, and the tech giants go to great lengths to find and attract them.

Modelers understand that models frequently have more than one solution. For economies, economists call these *fixed points*: a set of prices that replicate themselves. At a fixed point, supply and demand are equal everywhere throughout the economy. However, nothing guarantees that a particular fixed point is socially desirable. There may be multiple fixed points with very different social implications. Getting from one fixed point to another can be very, very hard.

An illustration may help make this point. Consider XYZ, a house painter who is four times faster at painting houses than the average for all house painters. What should XYZ be paid? Four times as much as the average because that is the value delivered? The same because XYZ works the same amount as other painters? There are people who would argue for either. It is socially acceptable to pay more, however, because everyone can see and recognize the added value. In the special case that is the real world, XYZ works for a painting company and is probably paid more than the average (but not four times as much) for retention reasons. The real winner may be the company that gets to collect four times the fee.

Now change the situation slightly. This time XYZ is a software developer. Productivity is now thirty times higher. Unlike house painting, very few people can appreciate or even understand this productivity difference. One of the few analogues is a world-class athlete. Again, though, for the athlete everyone can see the difference. With software that is not possible. XYZ can earn the thirty times compensation by doing a startup. In almost any company other than a tech giant or an aspiring technology unicorn, senior management cannot fathom such a differential. The result is that the 30Xers migrate to the tech giants and startups, leaving the rest of the world with crossbows fighting lasers. The outcome is our world today. One can only wonder how large, traditional companies can succeed.

There is also a more subtle problem that most enterprises face: you cannot operate a modern organization without software, so you have to make do with what you can get. Thus, most of the world runs on software that is either outdated or bad or both. This means systems are fragile, difficult to change, and open to attack. If the world is dependent on software, and if software talent is scarce, then there is a frontier of complexity within which the world must live.

This is profound. David Brin, a noted science fiction writer, recently mused on Twitter that humanity may have created a society with more complexity than it can actually manage. Humans seem well adapted to a roughly right world, and that is what we had until the last decade or so. In a roughly right world, you build in buffers and caches to handle errors and omissions and uncertainty. You have lots of resiliency, but you are not at peak efficiency. In a world of digital perfection, efficiency goes up but resiliency goes down. Capitalism as we have it today may not optimize to the right point.

While Halstead Length is so profound in regards to software, its importance is ancient. It is the power of narrative, the ability to remember an enormous amount. The few aborigines in Australia able to navigate to every water hole in the Outback are as much a demonstration of Halstead Length as is the software genius of today. So too were the ancient priests who learned and sustained the oral traditions of their culture.

Scientists really have no idea why some people have a longer Halstead Length than others. Is it, for example, piano lessons at age eight or sentence diagramming at twelve? Who knows. More germane to our current predicament is this question: What happens if Halstead Lengths shorten?

ANSWER-SEEKING

Casual conversation often revolves around answers to questions, but the key is most often the questions—not the answers. The famous statistician John Tukey is known for saying sixty years ago, "Far better an approximate answer to the right question, which is often vague, than the exact answer to the wrong question, which can always be made precise." I once coined a Gresham's Law of Answers: Precise answers drive out vague answers regardless of the merit of the antecedent questions.

We all do this. It is human nature. Given a problem we convert it into an (apparently) easier problem. As a result, two people can think they are solving the same problem but in fact be solving very different problems. Each may stubbornly insist on his or her individual answer. Conflict follows. Businesses face this all the time. The method of resolution is well known.

1. Make sure everyone is on the same page. Make all assumptions explicit and keep a complete list. The more diverse the group involved, the better this step will be. You need both a truth teller and a moderator to keep this on track.
2. Look for possible solutions. List them without being judgmental.
3. Evaluate the solutions against the assumptions.
4. Iterate as necessary.

Sometimes you find there is no solution. Then you delete constraints and assumptions. Delete enough and there is almost always a solution. Sometimes the constraints that are deleted were never listed in the first place, and this is why step one above is so critical. This is where things can go badly wrong very quickly.

Traditionally, education (especially higher education) has trained students to solve problems. Survival if not success required as much. However, when Sergey Brin committed Google to organizing all the world's information, he created a new way to live life: answer-seeking instead of problem solving. He reinforced this by keeping the Google search box uncomplicated and open ended, a non-obvious decision at the time. Both brilliant decisions for Google, but (as with Facebook) it had profound external effects.

As Google has improved its search algorithms over time, the quickest and easiest way to solve a problem is increasingly to ask Google (or YouTube, owned by Google) for an answer. It all seems so obvious and simple. Again, what could go wrong?

There can be no doubt that answer-seeking does not develop longer Halstead Lengths. The smaller the Halstead Length, the more constraints have to be deleted. This is just math. The purpose of a diverse group is to make the collective Halstead Length as large as possible. This all can work beautifully with the right group culture. However, as the group gets larger, this task gets harder, so the social Halstead Length gets driven to that of the smallest member of the group.

This is what answer-seeking has done to us as a society. We have made average individual Halstead Lengths shorter, and thus have shortened our social Halstead Length as well. The consequences are profound. We can end up with diametrically opposing solutions to the same problem with each side fervently believing in the correctness of their position. Compromise at this point is impossible. Sound familiar?

Unfortunately, we are about to experience an order-of-magnitude increase in this challenge, all in the name of progress. Artificial intelligence as a concept has been around for over eight decades. Its potential impact is not a new phenomenon. In the 1970s, professor Joseph Weizenbaum at M.I.T. wrote a Fortran program called Eliza, which mimicked a therapist. If it did not know how to respond, it replied, "Oh?" If I remember correctly, he said it was about five hundred lines—not a very complex piece of software at all.

The impact was enormous. Articles were written about this being the end of psychoanalysis. Today we would see it as a primitive chatbot. One day, he went to ask his assistant a question. She was sitting at her computer terminal, and as he approached, she put her arms over the paper and said, "Professor, please. This is personal. I am talking to ELIZA."

She knew exactly what ELIZA was, for she had typed it in for him. He was so stunned by her reaction that he wrote a book, *Computer Power and Human Reason*, in 1976. I assigned this book in my Harvard class on Computers and Society. The issues it lays out remain, as we are still human beings.

As we will explore in the next chapter, the danger with artificial intelligence is that it can provide eloquent, persuasive answers that are just totally wrong. AI knows what it knows, and it assumes that is the definition of truth. AI can be a powerful tool, but if you are conditioned to accepting what the computer says as truth, the risks are enormous. Humans can solve incredible problems, but answer-seekers solve none. This is the existential question with AI.

ABSTRACTION LAYERS

Halstead Lengths matter for software as much as height does for basketball. Software is congealed knowledge. Every business, every organization, and every process runs on some combination of data, rules, and lore. Since the 1950s, these have been increasingly mediated by software. The demand for good software is almost limitless. The supply is not. There simply are not enough great programmers. Moreover, developing software is costly and time-consuming. Little has changed in fifty years. For an idea of how little, see the 1978 article in the Association for Computing Machinery's Special Interest Group on Software Engineering's journal *Software Engineering Notes* titled "Managing Software Development"—most of which still rings true.[1]

In the beginning, there was no software. If you wanted to use a computer, you had to enter instructions directly and reference memory with the numeric location. In the earliest computers, dials were used to do this. (Legend says this where the term "bug" originated—a moth could fly into a switch and cause errors.) Decades later, nothing has changed in one sense. The computer still runs machine instructions pointing to absolute numeric addresses.

What has changed is how those instructions and addresses are generated. We continuously generate new abstraction layers. An abstraction layer hides the complexity that is underneath it and presents a different view of the world. Software is then developed against this abstraction layer. Each successive abstraction layer has the goal of making it easier or better in some way to write software, enabling a broader pool of humans to develop it. This is how we have historically dealt with the shortage of talent. This is not costless. The higher the abstraction layer to which you write, the less efficient is the software—though as computers have become more and more powerful this loss in efficiency is inconsequential.

Twenty years ago, the late Dale Jorgensen addressed these issues in a study for the Board on Science, Technology and Economic Policy of the National Academy of Sciences.[2] The data strongly suggested that we gained productivity as the speed of microprocessors improved because existing software could simply run faster on cheaper computers. The laws of physics eventually put an end to this. There is the speed of light constraint.

We could (and can) build computers that process more in a given time interval, but only if they can do multiple things at the same time. The result was that we saw a slowdown in productivity growth because we needed new software to exploit that capability. This created a need for new abstraction layers.

The first abstraction layer, assembly language, was a huge step forward, but really a miniscule step in itself. Only a tiny population could think and write at that level. Next came programming languages. Fortran became very popular (FORmual TRANslator) for scientific applications and is still in use today. Bloomberg terminal is still Fortran-based. COBOL (common business oriented language) became the standard in commercial applications. It is still used far beyond what you would expect (a recent study put daily usage in 2022 at approximately 800 *billion* lines). Fortran arrived in 1957, and COBOL in 1959. Both succeeded in vastly expanding the pool of people who could write software.

Personal computers appeared in 1977 with the Apple II and a new world opened up. Communities soon developed around them, and business opportunities abounded. Dan Bricklin invented the spreadsheet in VisiCalc, an entirely new abstraction layer that enabled millions of people to write (admittedly simple) software. Steve Jobs tried to get people to understand that a personal computer was like a bicycle and not a tiny car. As always, technology found its own level.

Bill Gates and Paul Allen founded Microsoft and made another abstraction layer, BASIC, for personal computers. Bill Gates's mother sat next to the CEO of IBM at a United Way board meeting and asked him if her son could help their new personal computer project. A note was passed down in IBM, and a team was sent to meet them. They were most interested in an operating system called CP/M, but its founder famously went flying instead of meeting the IBM team. They went with Microsoft. Microsoft immediately accepted and went down the street to buy what became DOS. The rest, as they say, is history.

Microsoft followed DOS with Windows, better versions of BASIC, and eventually a framework called .Net. Their strategy was brilliant: focus on helping mediocre developers develop mediocre software. They did it well. Great accounting software, for example, lost out in the market to a swarm of BASIC programs oriented to specific niches. A consultant claimed that virtually all the applications for the original Apple Macintosh were created by the same group of fifty or so developers because that interface was so complicated.

Workstations were more powerful personal computers, and the common abstraction layer there quickly became UNIX, which came from Bell Labs. Around UNIX the theme became open systems, and the competing companies cooperated on making their abstraction layers compatible to be more attractive to application developers. The winner in this space was Sun Microsystems and its version of UNIX known as Solaris.

Personal computers and workstations are themselves built on an abstraction layer, the microprocessor. Ted Hoff changed the world of semiconductors with the Intel 4004. Prior to that, "programming" was done by assembling a collection of single-purpose chips on a circuit board. Hoff realized that he could make a cheap, small chip that could be programmed with software to replace that circuit board. The 4004 was replaced by the 8008, and the rest again is history. Each improvement in abstraction layers allowed more developers to create more software. It was and is a virtuous circle. More hardware power allows more powerful abstraction layers, which in turn require more hardware power as they expand. Sun introduced a further abstraction layer in Java, which could run on almost any device.

Today, more and more computing runs in what we call "the cloud," meaning on a network of computers run by Amazon, Microsoft, Google, Oracle, IBM, and others. Each invests heavily in creating an abstraction layer to attract and hold customers. The goal is to make it easy to join and as hard as possible to leave. Artificial intelligence is nothing more than another abstraction layer. Same with machine learning or even the metaverse.

Hardware gets ever more powerful, which enables more powerful abstraction layers, which allow for the more efficient creation of software by more people. In Galbraith's time, technology innovation was hardware; today it is software. The result is an order of magnitude increase in the pace of innovation—and thus disruption. There is no end in sight. Unfortunately, the fact that more people can build more software does not mean that the software is dependable or robust. The abstraction layer itself might be perfect (although it never is), but there is a very old saying in technology: garbage in, garbage out.

Software is congealed knowledge, but the knowledge comes from elsewhere. Software embeds a model, but every model (every last one) is by definition an approximation.

In that lies danger. Models give precise answers without complete context; that precision implies an accuracy that is illusory.

Moreover, because that software is now running on top of literally millions of lines of other software that makes up the abstraction layers (and today software may be multiple abstraction layers deep) few humans will know how it actually operates, and fewer if any humans will have an instinctive feel for how it will behave.

This is not a minor issue. Consider the algorithms used today to guide medical practice. They may provide valid and helpful information for the majority of the population, but very wrong for some. It is impossible to test for this. Models have to be seen as suggestions, not directions. But that is not human nature.

We have compensated for the shortage of high Halstead Lengths by rewarding those who can create abstraction layers for others less gifted to use. By now, we have billions of people using technology created for at most a few million. That is a tremendous accomplishment and has brought the world much. But not all of it is positive.

Now, almost as if on cue, artificial intelligence is adding another abstraction layer—an abstraction that feels and acts much like a human being. The AI which incited this fever, ChatGPT, is far from perfect, but it captured public attention rapidly in 2023. It was a long time coming. The underlying GPT software came from DeepMind, a London-based company purchased by Google in 2014. Version three was released in 2020. GPT stands for Generative Pre-trained Transformer, which makes it clear that it is primarily powered by mathematics.

With help from some engineers hired from Google, the company OpenAI trained GPT-3 on openly available internet data at a rumored processing cost of $20 million. Training is not nearly as simple as it sounds. It is art as much as science, but training is what creates the pseudo-intelligence. The human analogy is schooling, learning and upbringing. The goal for OpenAI is what is known as artificial general intelligence, which means the AI can train itself as it learns. This is a ways off. Some think it's impossible. It is difficult to be definitive.

The important point is that the AI knows only the information on which it was trained. It assumes that its limited data set is the sum of all existing knowledge, so any of these systems can confidently produce information which is totally incorrect. There are two ways you can modify the behavior of this sort of AI. First, you can tune it, incrementally training it. Second, you can include information in the prompt you give it. This is so important that jobs immediately appeared for prompt engineers with annual salaries of $350,000 to $500,000 per year. Nevertheless, without tuning and with simple prompts, ChatGPT has proven able to write speeches, papers, poems, novels, screenplays, school assignments, sermons, newspaper articles, ad copy, and letters as well as shown the ability to pass MBA, legal, and medical examinations.

The public at large is generally familiar with this type of abstraction layer. Anyone who watched the original Star Trek series saw it routinely. More recently, Alexa from Amazon, Google Assistant, and Siri from Apple have made it part of billions of lives. But ChatGPT offers a whole lot more. And it will only get better. GPT-4 is better than GPT-3. Cheaper computing and greater storage mean the training can be more inclusive. GPT is what is called a large language model (LLM) and is currently limited to text, but the ability to generate images is already there. GPT can write a script for a movie. Soon it will be able to generate one in its entirety. The actors will be able to emulate actual humans. We already have a problem with deep fakes—videos that look authentic but are not. Movies are taking humans and portraying them as younger or older than they are. "I will believe it when I see it" will no longer be a marker for truth.

Any AI, like any human, will know what it knows and nothing else. At the moment, it lacks common sense. It will have hidden prejudices and some obvious ones. It will be very difficult to evaluate, just as humans are difficult to evaluate. It will not be infallible. Yet within years it seems certain the vast majority of interactions in which we humans interact with the systems that dominate our lives at work and play will be mediated by an AI. The brilliant developer George Hotz observed on Twitter that in fifteen years artificial general intelligence (i.e., human equivalent) will be able to run on our phones, accelerating the path in which humans increasingly seem to be just an appendage to our devices.

There is one huge and very old obstacle to all this: copyright. What right does the owner of a large language model such as ChatGPT have to use your content to train the model? If it does so, what compensation are you due? We have answers to neither question. At one extreme, it could lead to fragmentation, in which every owner of copyrighted content makes it available only through its own trained or tuned LLM. However, if the common LLMs lack access to all copyrighted content, they will be inefficient and frequently wrong.

One obvious way society can deal with AI is as old as

economics: competition. Again, technology does not cooperate. The more material you can use to train the model, the better the model becomes, so small, new entrants usually have an inferior product. Do we really want just one company to dominate AI? This is not a game in which small players can compete. The existing large cloud vendors have huge economic advantages, which is why the Microsoft partnership with OpenAI is so important.

One can easily see a number of ways in which AI can be incredibly beneficial to our society and economy. Most human-friendly abstraction layers have always been winners, and so will AI. However, vast numbers of jobs for humans will disappear—jobs thought immune to automation (attorneys and accountants, for example). As with targeted advertising, AI will also give us greater ability to bend people's thoughts through very subtle means. Dealing with the challenges it poses will be difficult, as our governments generally lack both the skills and experience to quickly understand and digest the issues. We will live in interesting times.

THE DECLINING RELEVANCE OF NEOCLASSICAL ECONOMICS

Our 250-year-old neoclassical economics ideology is simply obsolete—and it has been made so by what technology has enabled. This is the work of no single event; on the contrary, it was many, often motivated by a public policy that had only noble intentions. What was that aphorism about the road to hell?

Take pension reform for example. After World War II, career success meant a job—often one job that lasted an entire career—and in it you worked for your pension. Now, since a pension is an unsecured liability of the company, it was only as secure as the business of that company. Given that most CEOs at the end of their careers retired with their pension as their largest asset, they managed their companies accordingly, in a low-risk fashion. Why would they put everything at risk at this stage in their careers? There was, in general, a low rate of discount. People looked to the future.

Pensions, though, struck reformers as evil. They seemed to make you captive to your company—and to create an underhanded way to overpay executives. So for forty years, defined benefit pensions have been on the way out. Replacing them are defined contribution schemes: retirement plans in which you accumulate assets in order to fund retirement, often with tax advantages. One notable exception to this is in government at all levels, which creates a growing wedge between the private and public sectors.

In the United States, tax deductions for executive compensation were limited by law with exceptions for performance-based compensation approved by the shareholders. This has generated an enormous increase in executive compensation through rewards of stock options and restricted stock grants. Executive compensation in a large company is now dominated by stock-based compensation, and stock-based compensation means management benefits from those strategies that boost stock price. Economists call this *moral hazard*.

Stock options have been around for a long time. But until forty years ago you had actually to hold the stock-at-risk for at least six months. Then, same-day sale was authorized. Now you could exercise your options and sell them on the same day. This was a truly transformational change, justified by the idea of spreading options to all or most employees. CEOs now had to accumulate wealth to fund retirement, and stock options were the principal means of doing so. They had, in other words, a strong personal objective to drive up the stock price. But their interest was likely to be strictly short-term. They could cash in directly, so they need not care about the future health of the company. This of course created an enormous incentive to do what is referred to as pumping and dumping.

At the same time, securities markets were going through enormous change. Today, stock indices are part of everyday life: the Dow Jones Industrial Average, Standard and Poor's 500, FTSE, NASDAQ... Originally, these were computed manually at the end of every trading day. But that changed in the 1980s. Engineering workstations in the 1980s brought the power to compute these indices in real time, then the data feeds to support their broadcast became available, starting with the Monchik-Weber Ticker 3. Now you could trade based on these real-time indices, and so-called algorithmic trading began.

Today the vast majority of trades are algorithmic—done entirely by software, without human intervention. What began as largely mechanical trading for index funds has become ever more sophisticated. Hedge funds emerged to make sophisticated bets based on software-implemented algorithms. Suddenly, the time to develop and release software mattered enormously. Not coincidentally, the highest-paid developers were on Wall Street. Steve Jobs's NeXT computers found a profitable niche. Modern investment banks today have more software developers than bankers.

Hedge funds would have been completely unimaginable to Smith or Ricardo. In them, a small team (only tens of people) manage billions, or even tens of billions of dollars in assets. Compensation is astronomical. Finally, in 2008, the US Internal Revenue Service hit a roadblock: individuals reported more than a billion dollars in employee compensation—it was a total that the IRS systems could not handle.

Note that this is simply employee compensation, not capital gains or interest or dividends. The tried-and-true formula is 2 and 20: an annual management fee of 2 percent on all assets plus a "carry" of 20 percent of all gains. Although there is nothing at risk, the carried interest rule grants these earnings capital gains treatment. US politicians constantly challenge this rule, but they never change it, for the simple reason that their donor base benefits massively. Principles and self-interest do not coincide.

Paid to Gamble

The value of a company is always subjective, and the future is unknown and unknowable with any precision. Accounting would say that its value is the future value of the cash payouts that it will generate: simple in theory, but difficult in practice. Today, public companies are valued according to earnings-per-share and the price-to-earnings ratio. Private companies are valued by EBITDA (earnings before interest, taxes, depreciation, and amortization), which is a good proxy for cash generated, and cap rate or multiple.

There are voluminous rules that govern the calculation of earning-per-share for a public company, but this is all about precision, not accuracy. Market value to book value ratios have been increasing over time because more and more of the assets of a firm are intangible and not included on the balance sheet. Stock-based compensation was originally not included in the calculation of earnings, so company results were highly misleading. There was some rationale for this, but it did mean that profits were overstated. Regulators required change, but today the rules still significantly understate cost. Moreover, technology companies in particular love to ignore stock-based compensation in their reports. As long as they keep growing, investors do not care.

At the same time, the stock markets became more and more like a giant casino in which stocks were traded based upon anticipated gains and losses more than upon fundamental values. The epitome of this is what is euphemistically called "high-frequency trading." Though Michael Lewis captured this well in his book *Flash Boys*, the regulators never seemed to catch on. HFT—high-frequency trading— is just frontrunning. Nothing more, nothing less. The most valuable asset in the world for HFT was the physical length of the Ethernet cable that connected your computers to the network switch at the exchange. The shorter the cable, the more it cost. The reason was entirely clear: the speed of light is a constant. Tiny fractions of a second are still plenty long enough for a computer to take substantive action.

HFT systems paid to get an advance look, measured in milliseconds, at trades on the exchange. The advance look came only because you had a shorter cable. It was very brief, but it was enough. As soon as computers could move sufficiently fast, you could guess that someone wanted to buy a lot of a certain stock. Using your advance look, you then bought up all other offers to sell before reoffering them to that buyer with a slight markup. This practice made billions and billions of dollars per quarter for the major players.

A published report claimed that at a financial lunch ten or so years ago, one CEO began a talk by saying that unlike most people in the room he was a long-term holder. His average hold time for a stock was thirteen seconds. No one laughed. It cut much too close to the bone.

The 2008 financial crisis began in a similar way. Home mortgages had been a backwater at investment banks, which made money on leverage. More leverage meant more profits. Enter the concept of value-at-risk accounting. All financial institutions are required to hold assets in reserve to protect against losses. This is known as the gross leverage ratio.

The banks argued successfully that against less risky assets they should be required to hold fewer assets in reserve, as defined by one of the major ratings agencies (for-profit firms paid to assign a rating). The US Securities and Exchange Commission agreed, and the investment banks were allowed to go from a gross leverage ratio of around 13 to one of around 38, with much tighter limits in terms of value-at-risk accounting. By politicians of all stripes this was hailed as regulatory simplification. Algorithms ruled the day.

Suddenly, highly rated assets became extremely valuable, because you had to hold almost no reserves against them. They were also scarce—the solution was to generate more of them, and the way to do this was simple: algorithms.

In rough terms, at that time generally 93 percent of home mortgages were eventually paid off. So the default rate was 7 percent. The banks created pools of mortgages and then sold off tranches in this pool. Details varied, and many pools were more complicated, but an approximate picture shows the pools divided into three tranches:

1. Tranche A was the bottom layer, and all defaults were charged to it, though it also received any residual at the end. This was the equity layer.
2. Tranche B was the middle layer, and it got charged only if Tranche A became exhausted. Its risk rating was slightly higher, and it paid slightly higher interest than Tranche C.
3. Tranche C was usually rated AAA. Home mortgages were in general low risk, and this tranche was protected

by the lower tranches—so it paid an interest rate that was appropriate for a risk-free asset.

The strategy was hugely profitable for the banks. If the mortgages had carried a 7 percent interest rate, you could finance 80 percent of it at 3 or 4 percent in Tranche C. The excess all went to Tranche A, and you collected handsome fees along the way. What could go wrong?

All it took to make this work was software—and running roughshod over laws regarding property transfers and notarization. The consequence of this was that most mortgages had no owner for nearly all of their life. There was·no one with whom to negotiate. In fact, a mortgage only had an owner when it defaulted or when it was paid off. Otherwise, it was in zombie land. Since the payoffs were so large, the incentives to have mortgages were very large too. As a result, underwriting standards evaporated. The fundamental assumption—that only 7 percent of mortgages defaulted—became an illusion.

Investment banks invariably lend long and borrow short—a practice that is highly profitable, but also risky. Though no one can know for sure, there were reports that when Lehman Brothers failed, their gross leverage ratio was around 45:1. Legally, it had to be below 38:1, but they got around this problem by inventing overnight transactions, where they sold and then bought back assets at 11:59 PM on the last day of the quarter in order to comply. When regulators do not understand computing and software, anything is possible. Regulators should have learned this with the Equity Funding scandal four decades ago.

Thus, today we have a world in which corporate management is paid to gamble. Paid to go for the gold. Paid to pump up earnings per share. Paid to hype expectations. Paid to get the company's stock price up before cashing out. And when things start going badly, a CEO simply blames his or her predecessor, on the reliable assumption that no one will ever be able to show that it was their actions that made it all inevitable. The very idea of stewardship is simply a historical oddity. *Caveat emptor* has become the religion of the stock market.

Failure, furthermore, has become much more comfortable—thanks to the emergence of another group of players: private equity. People in private equity are smart, aggressive, and cold hearted, to be sure. But they are not evil. They are simply arbitrageurs, and they are essential to capitalism. They do what boards of directors seldom do: they replace management. They neither like nor accept so-called legacy misalignment.

They all have cookbooks and they follow the recipes carefully. Usually they replace management and align it tightly to shared objectives. In general, they are much better at technology, so they update it. They use leverage, and they are frequently able to take cash out of the business through debt. They take advantage of being private and clean out the balance sheet. The goal is to either sell or return to being public in three to seven years. It is a formula that works. The likely prospect of gains allows them to recruit talent that would otherwise be unaffordable.

For the failing management team, stock-based compensation usually makes this type of transaction quite profitable. Private equity firms probably have to pay 30–40 percent above the current market price, so there is value in all those options. Moreover, the options increasingly vest upon a change in control, so the executives leave in return for at least a few years of compensation to cushion their transition. Financially, no one wins from trying to fix a company, except perhaps the shareholders.

All of these changes have worked to create a robust venture capital sector, which is another form of private equity. Here the funded companies are smaller, and most of them fail. However, a small number succeed wildly. Given that initial prices to invest are low, the returns can be massive.

If you have an idea for a business today, the financial rewards come from creating a business, then selling it or taking it public. The capital is there to fund you, and with the exception of the technology giants, most firms have no way to compensate you equivalently. Venture capital means that the best and brightest leave big companies.

Without the financial crisis of 2008, there would be more natural limits on private equity and venture capital, but governments worldwide maintained artificially low interest rates for years thereafter in an attempt to start over. Go back to the beginning of this chapter. Retirement requires that you accumulate assets, for which you need return. As a result, pension plans and individuals see ever fewer opportunities to invest—they must allocate more and more to private equity and venture capital. The assets in the public market are bid up, because there are no alternatives.

All of this is a house of cards. As interest rates increase, we will find out how fragile the world is. There are policy changes that would help, but any of them would inevitably cause a one-time drop in asset prices. That is tough for any politician to stomach. A sales tax on securities transactions (that is to say a "Tobin tax," named after economist James Tobin, who first proposed it) would change the dynamics and cause the focus to shift to fundamentals. Eliminating the capital gains treatment on carried interest would reduce the unwarranted subsidy to private equity firms and venture capital. For a short time in 2022 this was on the table in the United States, but it was withdrawn. These are difficult issues. What is clear is that capitalism today is not the neoclassical economics of Smith and Ricardo.

TECHNOLOGY: DISRUPTER IN CHIEF

We live in a time when technology is changing faster than it ever has. It is a time when, in what seems like a flash, a new product becomes outmoded and is superseded by one that is yet newer and more advanced. It is a time when our means of doing the routine activity of our lives is transformed, and will be again and again. It is a time when technology itself might fairly be described as the disrupter in chief. It obliges change, while the rest of society scrambles to keep up. The pandemic has disrupted things to be sure, but even now technology is the vector that enables that disruption.

Moore's Law

Gordon Moore, a co-founder of Intel, mused in a trade publication in 1965 that the improvement of semiconductors seemed to double every eighteen months. We call this Moore's Law.[1] This translates to a 30 percent improvement in price performance every year, the fastest rate of productivity improvement that has ever occurred in human history. That's a 97 percent cost savings every decade.

In recent decades this dizzying transformation has come to seem quite normal, even as it continues to accelerate. The exponential rates of progress predicted by Moore's Law have held true for more than half a century. The internet, email, social media, the smart phone, "bots," cryptocurrency, big data, and AI: the world now, one-fifth of the way through the twenty-first century, is unquestionably a very different place from the one in which we grew up.

For countless generations, however, the world, and the technology in it, were entirely static. Galbraith might have declared change the law of economic life, and in modern times, of course, it long has been. But for most of human history—as he certainly knew—it wasn't. Fully 99.5 percent of this history was lived in the Paleolithic Era. In that time the world that people were born into was in almost all respects the same as the one they left when they, or even their grandchildren, died a century or so later.

Our interest here though is not with that 99.5 percent or even with the great majority of the 0.5 percent. It is with the very recent past, with the present and with the short-term future: with our own lifetimes and those of our children and grandchildren.

The unprecedented technological change that has occurred in recent years has taken place at a level impossible for the state even to monitor, let alone for it to tax or regulate. We're not talking about railroad companies, operating nationally. We're talking about things happening internationally and remotely, outside any real jurisdiction, crossing every border, in a "cloud"—things that we are attempting to monitor, to shape, and to control using institutions based on a world of nation-states, which themselves emerged in a much earlier and altogether different world. We're also talking about things written in a programming language that few speak, a language that is barely understood (or not understood at all) by the great majority of the legislators sitting in national parliaments, many of whom are attorneys trained to think very differently.

One central consequence of increasing the importance and centrality of technology in modern business has been, and will continue to be, the concentration of power, from wider to much narrower holdings: to the tiny percentage of the population able to comprehend and advance that technology. Only a handful of individuals have written the major operating systems used globally. From Dave Cutler, whose team created the foundation for the modern versions of Microsoft Windows, to Bill Joy, whose Berkeley Unix has evolved into the now-ubiquitous Linux, the exceptionally skilled technologists who have built the world's most complex systems are exceedingly few. The very small number of leading tech companies with which they are associated then recruit the majority of other workers globally who are also able to handle this complexity. This is partly about compensation, but partly too it is simply about the satisfaction of working with other highly talented individuals. Other companies are unable to compete: unable to promise the same rewards, financial or otherwise.

Now, even at the time that Galbraith was writing *The New Industrial State*—half a century ago, so comparatively very recently—he saw technology becoming both increasingly pervasive in society and sufficiently advanced to fundamentally alter the nature of modern capitalism. Only a couple of years after Gordon Moore made his famous prediction that semiconductors would decline in cost at a rate of 30 percent per year, this was a time when a few (but only a few) foresaw something of the huge impact that technology would make on the world. Galbraith was one of them, and what he foresaw was by no means entirely an improvement. The lives of humans would be transformed, while a global elite would use technology to accumulate both wealth and power: developments that have indeed taken place, just as he predicted.

The Startup Economy

In its essence, Galbraith defined technology as "the systematic application of scientific or other organized knowledge to practical tasks."[2] It was not, he said, synonymous with machinery, though it did very often involve it. But it was also more than this, and humans failed to appreciate this at their peril. Those books for children, he pointed out, that portrayed business life with reference to simple examples of commercial activity (one he cited showed a group of children selling glasses of lemonade while sheltering from the sun in the shade of a tree) were only actually considering smaller, older, and more traditional proprietors—proprietors who formed what was a diminishing fraction of the modern economy. To understand only this, he cautioned—this fraction of the economy that was "most nearly static"—was to understand, in fact, "very little." Actually, these books ignored entirely what was the economy's most significant and most dynamic portion, a portion quite different and less picturesque. And not different simply in terms of degree, but qualitatively, in a manner that invaded "every aspect of economic organization and behavior." This central element in modern society consisted of those "massively capitalized and highly organized corporations" that completely dominated the industrial system, what he described as the New Industrial State.

Today, that seems somewhat dated; startup companies have driven much of the innovation. However, in life-cycle terms, a few of these startups have become Meta (Facebook), Apple, Amazon, Netflix, and Google (known collectively as FAANG) . . . and countless more have been acquired by the giant companies Galbraith described. In Galbraith's time, capital was the constraint on technology as computing was very expensive. In modern times, talent is the constraint as computing has continued to get ever cheaper.

Galbraith reckoned that there were only several hundred of these large entities in the world, and his reckoning seems still roughly right. For these entities, the use of technology involves substantial investment, often in the form of an acquisition, and a growing time lag between the beginning and the completion of any task—"between any decision to produce and the emergence of a saleable product."[3] This time lag inevitably involved considerable investment. That investment still includes capital, but much investment today involves sustained operating losses while the business develops.

In World War II, Galbraith observed that "no combat plane that had not been substantially designed before the outbreak of hostilities saw major service."[4] This was a time when the premium and the incentive for such development could not have been higher. Since then, not surprisingly perhaps, the lead time has only grown.

Startups today provide the perfect economic model for the large corporations. The operating losses required in the early stages of building a new business are not on their profit and loss statement. The costs are lower because they have much lower overhead and frequently can pay less. Quality can be lower because consumers expect less of a startup than a major brand. Funding is provided by third parties.

What makes this work is that the large corporations pay handsomely when they eventually acquire the startup, and its investors and employees profit accordingly. To the corporation, the acquisition is a balance sheet expense that makes it far easier to manage with its shareholders. Indeed, for decades accounting allowed the pooling of interest mergers in which companies were magically assumed to have been merged all along. AOL and Cisco in particular exploited this in their rise.

To Galbraith, this economic fact of life was something with which only larger companies were financially able to cope. It involved the employment of a wider range of increasingly specialized manpower, each skilled at the increasingly subdivided (and decreasingly transferable) elements of an overall job. The result was the emergence of the large business organization, able to deploy the requisite capital, mobilize the requisite skills, influence the world around it (in terms of dictating the prices and wages at which it buys and the prices at which it sells), and cope with the substantial time lag between planning and ultimate sale: "between any decision to produce and the emergence of a saleable product." At the time he wrote, this was a very accurate portrayal of the world, and the paradigmatic example was IBM. But it ceased to be true over time, gradually but inevitably.

The trouble is that, just as Galbraith warned, the increasingly long period of gestation imposed by modern technology requires "greater certainty of markets." But instead of greater certainty, as timespans lengthen the opposite occurs, and reliability is lost. Look at contemporary events for instance—at the vast impact of Covid-19 on global economic life. This pandemic has only reemphasized the difficulty of operating as a company across a large timescale without either huge resources or substantial governmental support. The unpredictable can jeopardize the most careful planning.

Missile or Moon?

It is a fundamental fact that while the human brain can deal with ambiguity—can make presumptions, or fill in the gaps—computing "intelligence" simply can't. So while "roughly right" was good enough in the past because it was good enough for human brains, in a world of computers it no longer is.

We see this for instance in the military. At key moments in the Cold War, warning systems relied upon a human being to hit the override button when the rising of the moon or a misinterpreted domestic flight (both incidents based in reality) might have led a computer to instigate an automatic and devastating retaliatory attack. In both of these cases a human being was able to weigh the evidence and decide on balance that a genuine attack was improbable.

Also during the Cold War, examples provided a very clear illustration of the advantages and disadvantages of deliberate imperfection. In the Soviet army of a few decades ago, their helicopters or their machine guns, for instance, were basically designed to be (or in any case were in reality) imperfect and inefficient, but robust. So while the oil leaked in Soviet-era helicopters, the machines worked. They did shake. The pressures did vary wildly. After every flight the oil did need replenishing. But they worked.

The AK-47 likewise. It was, no doubt, a less accurate weapon than its Anglo-American equivalents. But you could bury it in the desert. You could bury it in mud. You could bury it in permafrost. Then you could dig it up—and it still worked. By contrast the American M-16, at least in its early days, or the British Army's SA-80, were much more temperamental, and jammed persistently. This was a problem much more likely to be fatal for the soldier concerned than would be a marginal inferiority of aim or an oil leak. In a shooting situation, without any hesitation, you would take reliability over a small degree of inaccuracy.

The importance of this is that the first 90 percent of

any task—the "roughly right"—is much easier than the final 10 percent that gets you to perfection. It is not just 10 percent more effort that gets you from 90 percent right to 100 percent right. It is triple that. Or quadruple that. When people tried to remove rats from an island off the French coast, they found it relatively straightforward to trap and eliminate perhaps the first 95 percent of the rodents. The final 5 percent, however, were extremely difficult. But in this case of course 95 percent really is no good, because if you don't remove 100 percent of the rats, the population will soon return to its previous level. This is also the reason why legal contracts (which have to consider and to allow for the most remote contingency) are so wordy, so time-consuming to create, and ultimately so little read.

Computers or systems are the same—just like the lawyers who need every *t* to be crossed. They too need even the most remote contingency to be considered and allowed for. The "roughly right" on which the human race has always operated quite happily, and which you can achieve in a fraction of the time, is not any good for them. With the birth of the modern, technological world, there has been a fundamental shift.

The fact that computers are now involved in most things—and will increasingly be involved—makes it necessary that we operate just like them. We can adapt. They cannot. This, it is important to understand, is a shift that massively privileges a very small percentage of the population (just like the lawyers who don't mind wading through pages of legalese). It massively privileges, too, those few big companies who are able to employ the great majority of these few, very highly qualified people.

We actually saw this some time ago in the US after the *Challenger* space shuttle disaster of January 1986. This infamous event occurred because of two 50-cent parts: the O-rings. And though the possibility that they might fail in the unusually cold temperatures that then prevailed at Cape Canaveral had occurred to some of those who worked on the project (and though engineers did raise the issue with their managers) nobody senior spoke out, for fear of jeopardizing, for the sake of two 50-cent parts, a mission that had cost more than a billion dollars.[5]

In the aftermath of the disaster, the pendulum has swung entirely the other way. Now we are obsessed with quality at all costs. The 100 percent has become right, and the increasing prevalence of computers has added enormous impetus to this development. Ninety percent is nowhere. "Roughly right" is wrong. Perfection is obligatory.

This is a fundamentally different way of working,

and one that forces revisions upon the whole of human society—technology is the disrupter in chief.

ALGORITHMIC SCALE

The Xerox Palo Alto Research Center is the source for much of the fundamental technology on which the modern world operates, beginning with Ethernet, the protocol over which we transmit information. Its inventor was Bob Metcalfe, but he will be more remembered for Metcalfe's Law: the value of a communications network is proportional to the square of the number of its users. Later researchers believe this is overstated, but that does not matter here.

Neoclassical economics depends upon competition or at least the threat of competition to hold things in check. Competition requires many things, but fundamentally there cannot be increasing returns to scale. If there are, the result is a monopoly, and no one argues that monopolists will behave. Yet, Metcalfe's Law in almost any form means that increasing returns to scale are the norm, not the exception.

It was over a decade ago that Marc Andreessen first said that "software is eating the world," and today, while some of the world still sits temptingly on a plate, the meal continues, software's appetite shows no sign of abating, and great chunks have been digested already.[1] Five years earlier, in 2006, the US National Academy of Sciences had explored the same idea in depth, in its project on measuring and sustaining the new economy.[2]

Today the dramatic shift is well advanced and completely unstoppable. Society has already been transformed, and stands in time (though in quick time given the scale of it) to be reshaped more fundamentally and more rapidly than it has ever been before, perhaps in human history. It is software, fundamentally, that is doing this reshaping. The pace of change has only been accelerated of late by the Covid-19 pandemic.

The shift is universal. Everybody needs software. It is endlessly malleable; it can be adapted for any purpose. It is immutable, in the sense that it lives for a very long time, if not forever, unlike poor organic creatures like us human beings who soon do, as Hamlet put it, shuffle off this mortal coil. In consequence, its financial returns are pretty much unlimited. Those who would legislate in order to control software companies—the would-be regulators—are in reality so far behind these companies that it is very hard to see how, in the near future, they could possibly catch up.

Power and wealth become ever-more concentrated because only a tiny minority of humans are capable, even with the right education, of conceiving and writing this software. The very small number of companies who understand the benefits that this talent brings can afford to reward it competitively, and are able to provide it a convenient and congenial environment, have been able to capitalize.

In the early days of the internet, people talked about a large company expecting to have 100,000 users. At the time this seemed like a vast number. Today, Facebook has over four billion users, and there are double-digit numbers of businesses with over a billion. A mere 100,000 is nothing: chickenfeed. The important point, though, is that software can be adapted to cope with any number. The scale of it quite simply takes one's breath away. It can, in fact, be practically infinite. The essence of cloud computing is that your computing environment is defined entirely by software. Hardware considerations have all but evaporated.

Boris Mouzykantskii—a theoretical physicist before he was a pioneer of modern technology—is considered the godfather of the online advertising industry. Dr. Boris (as many call him) invented what is known as *programmatic advertising*: the buying of online space when it is first chosen by computer, or by algorithm. So revolutionary has the procedure been that these days, prior to the Covid-19 pandemic, it was racking up around a trillion transactions per day. A trillion.

Car + Software = Phone

Now every industry has been penetrated by software and is being fundamentally transformed in a similar fashion. Perhaps you remember the days when people tinkered with and fixed their own cars? Not anymore they don't (unless the cars concerned are vintage or classic). Modern vehicles are run by software: not merely the engine but also the navigation, as well as all entertainment and safety features. Not to mention of course the fact that vast resources, and vast efforts, are being devoted toward dispensing with the driver altogether. Foxconn has created a car assembly line that can make most any electric vehicle on demand. The only thing they do not supply is the software.

Elon Musk has bet that in the race to fully automated driving, what his car manufacturer Tesla needs is faster chips (as opposed to more sensors) in order to match and supersede human eyesight. Existing computers, he discovered, are simply not fast enough at processing visual information. Generally, the answer to this has been additional sensors, and most car companies have been adding them to their vehicles. But Musk has argued that Tesla would not need them if only it could process video information faster: if, that is, it possessed faster chips. Should he be right, the consequences will absolutely devastate the traditional car industry.

A Tesla is really just an iPhone with a bigger battery and four wheels. It is controlled by software, just the same as an iPhone. And (like an iPhone or like much else in modern life) it is simply not amenable to hobbyist DIY. No more heads under the bonnet, in other words, unless in a workshop. But since it is essentially a computer, like a phone or a laptop, the software at the heart of a modern car can also be updated "over the air" (OTA) while the vehicle itself sits in the (private) garage or in the parking lot. A small change to the suspension? A minor but important alteration to how the car behaves? Neither requires a time-consuming visit to the repair workshop. Tesla owners can go about their day while the car fixes itself. But whereas, at Tesla, all of this is old news—and OTA has been around for a decade—a huge, old-fashioned car manufacturer like Ford, by contrast, has only just announced it. Nothing illustrates better what a gulf exists between Tesla on the one hand and the older automobile manufacturers on the other.

From cars to television, from books to the military, and even to agriculture, the world now operates not according to human rules but according to those dictated by software. Industry after industry has been or is in the process of being colonized and conquered.

As all business becomes software, the only real constraint becomes the cost of computing. And computing, of course, is vastly cheaper for a tiny number of major computing companies. It is the omnipresence of software that explains the enormous power of the technology companies that produce it. The process is circular, and is very hard to break.

In order to understand the power of a company like Amazon, one must understand that what it is not is a vendor of books, or music, or films, or groceries. To be sure, it is all those things. But what it is essentially is a computer company—and with that, it can go anywhere. Industry lore holds that at a strategy session back in 2003 Jeff Bezos emphasized (entirely correctly of course) that what his company did best was to build and operate complex software. Look at Amazon Web Services, a rapidly growing and immensely profitable arm of Amazon's operation—accounting for half of the company's enormous operating income—which focuses upon the provision of cloud computing platforms to everyone, from individuals to large companies and governments. What their immense computing power enables Amazon to also do is process and glean advantage from the huge quantities of data that it is able to accrue. As James Thomson, a former Amazon executive observed: "They happen to sell products, but they are a data company."[3]

In all of the vast and seemingly random intricacies of customer behavior, they are able to find patterns, and to make useful predictions, which inform and affect their conduct as a business. Their fundamental realization was that, whatever the idiosyncrasies upon which we pride ourselves, people on aggregate are in fact very predictable—and this is what allows them to ensure, for instance, that they have something in stock when we happen, quite by chance, to need a replacement for an old one that has worn out a certain number of months after we purchased its predecessor.

What the strength of Amazon shows, furthermore, is by no means atypical. On the contrary, its practices are nothing if not grounded in the careful study of human behavior. In the past, railroad companies lost because they thought, mistakenly, that they were in the railroad business. Wax paper people have lost because they thought that they were in the wax paper business. Wrong in both cases! What in reality every business needs to understand is that what they are really in is the information processing business, and what this means today is the computing business.

Over thirty years ago, I heard Dr. Craig Fields, who had just been the director of the Advanced Research Projects Agency of the US Department of Defense, speculate that in ten years the movement of information about goods and services would be more important than the actual physical movement. How right he was. How radical an idea it seemed at the time.

Everyone needs software. Not only are all companies information processing systems, human lives have become information processing systems, which is why everyone—all over the world—now carries a smartphone. What the smartphone is doing to all of our lives has happened already in business, and so those who design, produce, and maintain this software are in an immensely powerful position—a "narrow priesthood," as Harvard professor Shoshana Zuboff has described them—presiding, in what seems a stratified, unbridgeable, feudal fashion, "at the pinnacle of a new society."[4]

No wonder, therefore, that the major supermarkets are so apprehensive about Amazon's entry into the grocery sector. Not only does Amazon have no need to make a profit until it has established a position of market dominance—a tactic it has used before, of course, without the vast financial reserves it has accumulated since—but its computing power (and the comparative low cost, for Amazon, of computing) means that it is more than capable of completely restructuring and remaking a large, established industry sector like groceries. Walmart in the US, Tesco in the UK, and all the others, had better watch out.

Bookselling, of course, was also a large, established sector, and look at the impact Amazon has had upon it. The company has enormous power—and its power is very frightening for its competitors (even the large and established ones) who do need to make a profit and who will therefore struggle to compete on price.

In comparison with most other technology companies, Amazon has a very different culture, and a key part of this culture is huge rewards for those who are driving its computing energies, upon which the whole edifice is constructed. The grocery sector—populated as it is by enormous and well-established major players, but major players that are supertankers, which turn neither quickly nor easily—stands to be invaded and completely overhauled. Nerves, in the circumstances, are justified.

Monopoly Guys

What does this all mean for the viability of competition? For more than two centuries, the idea of the importance of competition has lain at the heart of economic analysis. Adam Smith himself wrote, "in general, if any branch of trade, or any division of labor, be advantageous to the public, the freer and more general the competition, it will always be the more so." The assumption has been that where competition exists, in a bid for customers, then prices of goods, commodities, or services will be lowered, and that the quality of customer care will rise. In both cases this will be to the obvious advantage of consumers. Any company failing to match its competitors will lose business and may ultimately go out of business. To this the general view has been: good riddance. The customer stands only to benefit.

It has been believed, furthermore, that any market dominated by a very small number of large companies is likely to be less competitive, and therefore less good for the consumer, than one consisting of a much larger number of small to medium-sized ones. Large companies are often older, more set in their ways, and saddled with a fixed culture less likely to innovate. Large companies, Galbraith observed, are driven most by their need to survive as organizational entities.

Monopoly in particular, furthermore, has been deeply tarnished by the experience of state-run enterprises in the communist world of the USSR and Eastern Europe—inefficient, unresponsive behemoths, desperately lacking the rigors and efficiencies instilled in an open market by smaller, leaner, sharper competitors. They have been presented as exemplars of what competition, or the lack of it, can do, both to attitudes and to practices.

The reality in the modern tech world, however, has in fact been—or seems to be—precisely this: large monopolies. Google, Amazon, Facebook, and Tencent are companies with no obvious competitors—not since they beat their would-be competitors into the dust; perhaps the reader is old enough to recall searching the internet on a search engine other than Google. One of the consequences of technology is that it accelerates this trend toward monopolies, and once companies do become unchallenged leaders, it is well-nigh impossible to dislodge them from what is often a monopolistic position.

One could not, though, accuse Amazon, or Google, or

Facebook, or Apple of incompetence. They do not invite the sort of jokes—the sort of derisive and (strictly nostalgic) affection—that did, say, the old British Rail or the East German Trabant car: icons of bloated, nationalized unreliability. In the case of the Amazons, or the Googles, they are more likely to be accused of ruthless efficiency than the opposite. (As legal scholar Lina Khan has noted, customers are inclined to approve wholeheartedly: something that was rarely said about British Rail or Trabant. We should not, though, be lulled into a false sense of security; modern, technological capitalism, Zuboff also warned, "gives so much, but it takes even more.") In spite of their efficiency, these tech companies—in significant areas at least—can easily become monopolistic.

Far from operating willingly alongside competitors, they can use their economic power and their position of market dominance to force rivals out of business. Amazon Trader provides perhaps a semblance of competition, a fig leaf (and Amazon is undisguisedly pleased to announce that these third-party sellers are now selling more in aggregate than is Amazon itself). But it is Amazon who owns the portal, Amazon who amasses and holds onto all of the valuable data on customer preferences and practices, Amazon who acquires customer loyalty, and Amazon whose brand is reinforced. And it is Amazon who, needless to say, takes a cut of the sale price.

This is no sort of competition that Adam Smith would have recognized. Amazon not only in essence organizes the tournament, owns the pitches, and enters a team, but it has even established the rules by which the game is run: Would people be happy were a World Cup to be organized in this way? The company is not, clearly, competing with others in the marketplace as an equal party.

Amazon is quick to point out that it does face stiff competition in each sector of which it is a part, even if not by any one player across the board. In the grocery sector that it is now entering wholeheartedly, for instance, there are clearly some major and well-established companies. There are other large providers of film and television, including, in Netflix, one of the oft-mentioned FAANG organizations. There are also, of course, other large computing companies.

The Amazon model is actually very similar to that employed by Microsoft and Intel in the first decades of personal computers. A very competitive industry made and sold personal computers, but they all had to buy their processors from Intel and their operating system from Microsoft. Competition was a very thin veneer.

THE SOCIAL RATE OF DISCOUNT

Do we care about the future? This is not an abstract question, because it is the fundamental issue on environmental protection. How much current sacrifice are we willing to accept to guarantee future generations a better life? The general consensus seems to be not enough, as was proven by the 2021 COP26 conference.

In 1923, Frank Ramsey wrote an article in which he argued that a generation had no right, when making decisions, to discount the welfare of future generations who would necessarily experience the effects of them. Renowned for little else, Frank Ramsey's own guarantee of a long-term existence beyond his own death—of being widely remembered—stems ironically from his ideas about the rights of future generations.

People in the present, Ramsey insisted, had no right literally or metaphorically to spend on credit when doing so would present a future generation with the debt. He called this the Social Rate of Discount, and that term endures. Measurement of economic expense is factored over time, so that the wellbeing of future generations is taken into account alongside that of those alive (and adult) today.

Is there a morally legitimate rate at which the welfare of future generations can be discounted by the current as it makes decisions? Ramsey insisted that there was not: that the only legitimate rate of this discount was zero. Much more recently, Pope Benedict XVI issued an encyclical from the Vatican that made the same argument—that society has no right at all to discount the welfare of future generations. In *Caritas in veritate*, his third and final encyclical released in 2009, he argued that those with the power to do so should ensure that "the economic and social costs of using up shared environmental resources are recognized with transparency and fully borne by those who incur them, not by other peoples or future generations."[1]

We do need to take the future, and the fate of future generations, into account, even if—because they are infants or have not yet even been born—they do not have a voice to be heard or a vote to cast. At least since Alexis de Tocqueville wrote *Democracy in America* early in the nineteenth century, it has been recognized that an indifference to the long-term future beyond an immediate tomorrow is, as Tocqueville put it, completely brutish. One of the things that separates humanity from the animal kingdom is the former's ability to conceive of a distant future, beyond the welfare of one's immediate offspring. Only a keen awareness of our place in time, Tocqueville wrote, could lead to a mode of governance "great, permanent and calm."[2]

Since Ramsey's time, a number of economists have modified his line of thought a little. They have argued that, providing one generation is leaving its successor an expanding economy, the former can in fact discount the welfare of the latter at the growth rate—perhaps 3 percent a year—on the basis that in economic terms the lot of those alive now is very much better than it was for their distant antecedents. They can cope, it has been argued, with a small debt in return for what are very significant benefits.

The development of information technology in particular has made this "discount" much easier to stomach, precisely because it is so much harder to discount the welfare of the present generation when communication technologies—television, for instance, or social media— make the suffering of others so much more vivid: suffering worldwide, moreover, not merely local suffering. As the pain etched in people's faces is streamed to us from hundreds or even thousands of miles away, so the distance over which human empathy can operate has expanded enormously.

Concentrated immediate pain is amplified. Future benefit meanwhile—impossible to portray in anything like so poignant or emotional a way—is minimized. While all public policy inevitably involves a trade-off (money spent now on one thing is less money that can be spent now on something else, or less money that can be saved for some unspecified future usage) technology has tilted this awkward decision making decisively in favor of the present. It has massively increased our spatial breadth of awareness, but has decreased it in temporal terms.

As a result, there are and can be no major projects now that are comparable in timetable with, for example, the medieval construction of the great cathedrals. In this case, the architects—the early engineers or the builders— had no expectation whatsoever of living to see the project completed. What they did of course have, which a markedly smaller percentage have today, was a different rate of discount: a firm belief in an afterlife much more important than life on earth, and (for some) a firm belief that by honoring God in this way they would maximize the likelihood of eternal bliss in heaven, discounting time in purgatory or avoiding hell.

Compounding this issue is that no one can predict the future with certainty—assuming that neither star signs nor mediums offer any more reliable guide to prediction than tea leaves or animal entrails. Which is to say: none at all.

Soothsaying

Computer modeling is making progress. We now commonly use the phrase *machine learning* to describe situations in which a model is generated by analyzing the data. Sometimes, provided that the questions are kept narrow, the variables do become manageable. Short-range weather forecasts, for instance, are a great deal more accurate now than they were even a few years ago. The systems are better understood, and the models more complex and more reliable. The imminent arrival of quantum computing, with the massive increases in computing power it will bring, will certainly improve the business of forecasting future pathways within complex systems.

Already though, the days when one would be correct more often by simply assuming that the weather tomorrow will be the same as it is today (predicting stasis rather than change) have passed. And while it might be even harder to predict the weather on a particular day further in the future, scientists are confident that their data and careful modeling do allow them—within certain parameters—to predict future change to the broader climate.

As far as more general human prospects go, however, the potential variables are far too large. What will be the impact of climate change? Will it devastate economic progress? Will it make much of the world uninhabitable and plunge humanity into a new dark age? Or will technology find a solution for these problems—problems of its own creation—and enable further progress? Will the proliferation of increasingly potent weapons destroy human civilization, or will technology proffer a solution to this nightmare scenario? Will microcomputing, computers no bigger than molecules, be able to operate inside the human organism—offer a cure for disease as it is currently known? Will dramatic improvements in space travel raise the genuine prospect of humans living elsewhere in the universe, if our current home—Earth—was to become uninhabitable? On most sides of all of these questions, highly intelligent people are to be found; but, as with political loyalties, presumptions are as likely to be shaped by personality or predisposition as they are by analysis.

Consider the difficulty, and the dismal track record, of economic forecasting. Politicians (among many others) would love to know whether the economy will be thriving in five years' time—but at present they don't, of course, and can't. It is notorious that very few if any major economic recessions have been accurately predicted by those whose job it has been to study the economy.

The 1929 Wall Street Crash—about which Galbraith himself, of course, wrote a famous study—was little foreseen, with most "experts" considering early falls no more than a healthy correction and a fabulous buying opportunity. (The economist Irving Fisher might have been most reviled for his confident and subsequently infamous declaration that stock prices—shortly before their fateful and sudden descent—had reached "a permanently high plateau," but he was only one of many.)[3]

In truth few modern economists are now any more likely to want a reputation for foreshadowing gloom that fails to materialize—and few, as a result, anticipate it when it does. Galbraith's sensible advice was to avoid the business of prediction altogether, on the basis that people were likely to forget any wise forecasts and recall (vividly) only the inaccurate ones.[4] The truth, as Galbraith certainly saw, is that the economy of one major country—let alone an increasingly globalized and international economy—is far too large and complicated to predict with any accuracy. The extent to which this is true grows all the time, even as computing power expands enormously. We simply don't know how to measure the economy anymore. Technology has made our economies worldwide so intertangled that modeling has become nearly impossible.

The rule book according to which things are measured is hopelessly out of date. Those state bodies—the BEA (Bureau of Economic Analysis) in the US, the National Audit Office in the UK—that try even to track the economy in the present often lag years, perhaps a decade, behind reality. Massive events, whether global warfare or pandemic disease (to choose one rather topical subject), have a vast impact upon economic fortunes, but are of course almost impossible to predict.

In any case, as is now increasingly accepted, even in comparatively stable times, human beings certainly do not behave like the completely rational actors of economic theory. Unlike the latter, for instance, they may prefer not to relocate on demand according to the undulations of the job market when other factors—emotional associations, family and friendship groups—pull them in a different direction. All too often the dictates of economics are not predominant in the human psyche.

To some extent this idea is evident, and has long been taken for granted. When considering an expensive infrastructural project, for example—a new highway, or a new railway line—a routine cost-benefit analysis would consider its impact not only upon people in the immediate future but also upon people in the longer term. The impact of this sort of major project is certain to be long lasting.

To cite just one example, it can now be seen what a vast, long-term difference US president Eisenhower made by pushing through the interstate highway system in the US with the Federal Aid Highway Act of 1956—against widespread opposition. While this was clearly not the work of one man, it was Eisenhower himself who staked his considerable credibility to a long-term project few of whose benefits he lived to see for himself (Eisenhower died in 1969; it was not until 1992 that the completion of the network was proclaimed). It united American states, countering geographical distance in a way that perhaps only the construction of the railways or the advent of regular domestic flights has rivaled.

Once, it was relatively easy for those in Europe, say, to discount the pain caused by an African famine (or one in India, or anywhere else). Ignorance was almost total, and exposure to the suffering was effectively zero. To cite just one example, the Great Ethiopian Famine, which went on for four years between 1888 and 1892, did not, in spite of its dire nature, make a significant impression in Britain or in the US.

But since Michael Buerk's famous televisual reporting of the "biblical famine" in Ethiopia just under a century later—reporting that simplified or even eradicated entirely any awkward political causation—news organizations have been profoundly aware of the power of disaster footage. Viewing figures, and with them advertising revenue, increase markedly. The same thing happened across the US after Hurricane Katrina. The effect is to make it enormously difficult, politically, not to be seen to spend in the present in an effort to assist: harder, in other words, to protect funds for the benefit of future generations.

Short-Term Wins

The result of this is that we tend to focus upon fixing the short-term over a wider geographical range, without regard for what it means ten, twenty, or thirty years down the road. Politicians in the West are all becoming more like Bill Clinton has (rightly) been accused of being: obsessed with helping right now, to the benefit of his own short-term popularity, at the expense of society's longer-term health. Needless to say, there are plenty of social problems in western (and all) societies that cannot be fixed in a year or even in a few years. But it is only those that are politically attractive—only those whose results individual, active politicians can point to and say: "Look what I did." What is the motivation for elected politicians to vote for a program whose results might take fifty years to realize? This is perhaps one reason why the UK's House of Lords— exempt, as it is, from the usual, short-term democratic pressures—is still around.

Nothing has illustrated this development as potently as the pandemic of 2020. This has not been a disaster unique to democracies, of course: countries all over the world have been affected. But what can be seen, particularly in western democracies, is enormous (if understandable) popular, political pressure to spend extravagantly in an attempt to mitigate or alleviate the consequences. Vast expenditure and vast borrowing have been the result, with the consequences left to be borne by future generations. In Britain, even a Conservative government—more likely historically to lay a claim to financial prudence than the rival Labour Party—has led this policy, and its chancellor of the exchequer has reaped the political benefit in spite of plunging approval ratings for the government as a whole.

Interestingly, Tocqueville insisted long ago that this sort of short-termism was much more likely "amid the turmoil of democracy," in which the future was masked and any citizen's thoughts were "unwilling to go beyond the next day," than it was in an autocratic regime (with its "five-year plans," however misguided or fanciful they might be—not that he of course knew anything of the Soviet Union). While this is hardly a new phenomenon, the development of technology has exacerbated it significantly.

Changes in the wider economy have had a similar effect. Companies tend to be more mobile. Investments are made with an eye to returns in the shorter term. The clear tendencies of the recent transformation in executive pay, as discussed earlier, put little emphasis upon stewardship in the long term.

Another area in which the subject has been very powerful of late is that to which Pope Benedict alluded: the environment. He was talking particularly about resource depletion, about the potential exhaustion for instance of substances like oil, or rare elements, or the hunting or fishing of wild creatures to such an extent that far fewer of them will remain for the benefit or enjoyment of succeeding generations.

Global warming, though, is also an obvious case in

point. Here is a phenomenon caused by past and present behavior with the potential to impact future generations very significantly indeed—the consequences of the damage are not borne primarily (or at all) by those who are causing it. It is an area in which planning for the future is plainly vital to human welfare in the long term, and in which the government has had to impose economic incentives to innovation in the alternative energy sector in a way that is now bearing fruit—the costs of wind power, for instance, having fallen markedly in relation to fossil fuels.

But allowances for the long term, which people increasingly accept that we should make, are becoming—in the democratic world most of all—much more difficult, as it becomes harder and harder to ignore present demand. Both the democratic political system and commercial self-interest in the private sector encourage short-termism rather than thought or planning for any longer-term future.

For instance, it has often been noted that the demands of the electoral cycle place a clear term on the distance that democratically elected politicians (along with the civil servants who work for them) are likely to look or plan ahead. Bill Clinton is hardly an outlier. Although some issues or projects do require a longer-term view, most of the time it is barely beneficial for elected representatives to think beyond the next election, after which they may be in or out of office. Their clear interest is in encouraging people to vote for them in the short term—which they do by attending as much as possible to present concerns.

The unborn generation or those who are currently small children, have no vote and therefore no voice about which politicians feel any incentive to concern themselves. While people are aware of course of the interests of their children or grandchildren, these concerns—hypothetical, opaque, unknown—may struggle to weigh heavily in the balance against the pressing needs of the present.

As long as democracies operate by voting separately on each need, without any cap on overall spending, there is bound to be a constant majority in favor of taking care of all present needs without regard to budget. (The money that is spent, of course, is notional—it is not really, for voters, our money—and the truth of this becomes greater the further one moves from the center of political power.) To be fair, the UK is better at this as a result of the stronger role of the chancellor of the exchequer, which does impose a central cap.

Perhaps government might be modified by laws that impose an overall spending limit. Then, obviously, a debate could take place in a democracy about what exactly this limit ought to be. But such are the electoral pressures of which politicians are all too aware that it is hard to imagine any such limit remaining intact in all contingencies.

The irony is that while we in the western world spend a lot of time worrying about remedies for inequality—at least insofar as this stems from opportunity as opposed to outcome—this is just another form of inequality: an inequality between the living and the unborn, or between the old and the young (generational inequality). As technology and economic advancement allow us to fix more problems—to deal with more issues of healthcare or poverty—so it becomes harder and harder to restrict spending.

For people to request the best healthcare treatment is entirely understandable. We would all do the same. But it presents governments with a massive problem. Technology keeps improving healthcare interventions, just as it keeps raising their cost. We all know how illusory proved the belief that the costs of subsidized healthcare would decrease over time as the general health of the population improved—as was assumed, for instance, by the founders of the National Health Service in Britain. In fact the opposite has taken place. Expensive new drugs and treatments, combined with an aging population much more prone, during the (much elongated) last years of life, to require costly interventions, have pushed up the costs of healthcare exponentially.

Right now, of course, the issue of state spending on credit is particularly topical, because the spread of Covid-19 has led to widespread government spending, larger than any since World War II. The US national debt recently passed the $31 trillion mark. Across the world governments able to do so are happily footing the bill for expenses that would previously have been hard to imagine, thus driving up their national debts.

It is not easy, in an atmosphere of crisis, to conceive how this could be different. In an extreme situation like World War II, it could have been argued that massive spending on credit was justified by a situation in which free society itself was threatened. But the debts are no less real; future generations are saddled with them, and impoverished by them. While a general presumption seems to exist that we can spend freely now and let the consequences look after themselves, Ramsey and Pope Benedict would rightly point out the unjustifiable nature of this way of thinking.

Short-Term vs. Long-Term

And what of the private sector? Clearly the social discount rate is not exclusive to government—the tendency toward short-termism permeates modern society. It is true that in some cases planning is made for the future by private organizations. In the technology sector, for instance, massive companies with significant resources like Apple, Facebook, Amazon, and Google are investing enormous sums in capital enterprises with an eye to the long term: constructing data centers that require vast amounts of power, for instance, and the laying of enormous fiber optic cables. As Galbraith was well aware, large private companies have long been required to plan and to invest ahead. New cars or airplanes, for instance, must be designed with significant lead time.

Nevertheless, in general it remains true that efficiency trumps robustness and resilience in democratic capitalism. This, in essence, is a way of saying that the short term trumps the long term. Little precaution is often taken for a large-scale downturn, which, while it might be unlikely in the short term, becomes much more likely—in some form—the more time is allowed to pass. We just learned this with Covid-19.

The Chinese regime would argue, of course, precisely this: that democracy leads to excessive focus on the short term and that this makes it inherently undesirable. They would accept Tocqueville's argument. But this revolution requires informed human intervention—deliberate guidance—if it is to be made "beneficial." While (unlike the Soviet Union and its satellites during the Cold War, for example) modern China works through the market, it is precisely the role of the Chinese state not to be at the behest of short-termist popular pressure but to impose a longer-term vision—something they are now doing in force.

An unfettered market economy, were it permitted, does not, they might argue, have a future. However, the government's unwillingness to take account of the immediate impact of policies upon individuals has of course the significant downside that segments of the population—notoriously of late in the Uighur community or in Hong Kong—suffer for their opposition to broader policy.

THE END OF PRIVACY / THE RISE OF SURVEILLANCE

The concept of privacy is something that we are used to taking for granted. At the heart of modern life, as we in the western world have known it, has been the right to anonymity, the right to be forgotten, to disappear—"to be left alone." We are used to a distinction between public life and private life, a division that would have been alien to our ancestors only a century or so ago.

We should remember, though, that there is not anything inevitable or eternal about this idea of privacy. On the contrary, it is a concept that arose as the result of specific historical circumstances, and it has been under attack for many years now, gradually eroded by modern technology and its exploitation. Slowly but surely, privacy is being chipped away, and this process is near certain to continue. If privacy is something that we value, it is essential that we treasure it, guard it, and do not carelessly discard it purely for the sake of convenience.

The majority of the population enthusiastically embrace the many ways in which modern technology makes life easier. We love the fact that we can send near-instant emails, at minimal cost, to friends on other continents. We love the fact that mobile phones offer the ability to call anyone from almost anywhere, and to be contacted likewise. We love the near-unlimited access provided by the internet, to both information and resources, and the ease of keeping a network of family and acquaintances updated on social media. We love the ease of location and of route-finding using GPS technology.

I understand these advantages, I benefit from them just like everyone else, and I don't wish to be a prophet of doom. It is vital, however, that people are conscious of the implicit trade-off: vital that they know and accept that these advantages are not free. On the contrary, the privacy that my generation has always known, and on which we have come to depend, is gravely threatened by these technological developments.

I am not claiming that the threat is malicious. No

villain is plotting, with a cat lying on his or her lap, to enslave us. But sometimes well-meant changes do have an unseen, and unrealized, downside. And these changes have the potential to undermine liberty in a way that few might accept if they truly understood what it was that they were accepting. Snooping does not just happen in the real world. It happens in the virtual world too, and the consequences are no less damaging.

A History of Privacy

Privacy is not, as might be thought, eternal, but a comparatively recent invention. Before the nineteenth century—certainly before the Industrial Revolution, before urbanization—it simply did not exist. People lived in small communities of two or three hundred people. They were related to most of these people and knew almost all of them. Go back to the medieval period, say, and the majority of people who were not particularly rich lived with their entire family in a single room: what we might now regard as an extended rather than a nuclear family. How could what we consider privacy have existed?

Even at the top of the social ladder, for royalty, the lives of the king and queen would at all times have been very public by modern standards. In the bedroom. In the toilet. The office of "Groom of the Stool" combined what seem to be the most degrading tasks with almost unparalleled access, which bequeathed great power. (The word *privy* has retained this double meaning as privy counselors know.) Royal bedrooms had railed-off spaces, and viewing platforms, where homage could be paid, even if it is true that there were often separate public and private bedrooms.

Ambassadors and other esteemed dignitaries might be received, there being no sense that a bedroom was an inappropriate place for such official business to be conducted. While it was certainly true that only very select individuals could gain entry to the inner sanctum of any palace, access was not controlled according to any notion that we would recognize as "privacy." The King asleep. The Queen in childbirth. Neither was any more "private"—in the modern sense—than are pandas in a zoo. They, just like the pandas, lived public lives.

Or consider the system of trial by jury that emerged in England during this period (perhaps with Scandinavian roots). What we are apt to forget is that this was not, in the early days, a trial by twelve good men and true who were strangers. On the contrary, jury members lived in the same small community as the accused. They were quite familiar with him or her. Unlike today, they did not simply listen to the details of an investigation carried out by others. They themselves were responsible for discovering the facts—for investigating—themselves. And, knowing the accused, they began this process with a clear presumption of guilt or innocence based upon knowledge of his or her past behavior, which would be as likely to decide a verdict as the facts of the case in question. They had the very information about prior convictions that has often been considered inadmissible on the basis that it would be too liable to influence a jury's decision.

So what changed? First, and formative, was that notion of the individual human being upon which is premised so much that has come afterward. It would be easy to assume that this too is eternal and inevitable. In fact, though, it owes its origin to perhaps the only technological development of the last millennium—the only revolution in communications media—as significant as the current internet revolution, responsible for the seismic transformation of the fifteenth century: the invention of the printing press.

As both information and ideas began to circulate more freely than ever before, the movement went unchecked by political boundaries, which proved completely unable to arrest the flow. As ideas moved, literacy spread—

the appeal of access to this information, and to these ideas, proving irresistible. With its privileged hold on intellectual property shattered, the grip of the elite began gradually to weaken. The power of long-established religious and political authorities was threatened. A "middle class" began to expand dramatically. The entire traditional structure of society was overturned.

As often, one major change fomented another. Without the unparalleled transformation brought by the printing press, it is impossible to imagine the vast impact made a century later by Martin Luther, in Wittenberg, as he hammered his Ninety-five Theses onto the door of All Saints' Church. It was the printing press that then transformed what would have been a relatively minor theological rebellion into a mighty, world-changing torrent.

The impact of these changes only grows with hindsight. Over time, the Roman Catholic Church was itself massively influenced by the Protestant Reformation. The Bible was translated, as never before in Western Europe, into local languages, rather than being preserved in a relatively inaccessible code (Latin), which required an intermediary—a priest—to decipher it. Every believer could read for him or herself the word of God, as it was written in His holy book.

While Martin Luther had presumed that everyone must,

inevitably, draw the same conclusions as had he from the text of the Bible, in fact the outcome could not have been more different. A massive fracturing of the Christian community took place. Not only did Protestants break from Catholics. Protestants themselves separated into numerous different denominations and creeds, as all manner of new reformers promoted innovative and inconsistent interpretations. From one person—one Pope—sitting at the head of the western Christian community (ignoring, for a moment, that the Orthodox Church—which had always translated scripture and liturgy into vernacular languages—had long since parted ways with Rome) came a complete and colossal splintering.

Along with mass communication, therefore, came the central concept of modern life and the modern world: that of the individual. As the tide of faith subsided, it was the individual human who was left standing alone upon the sand. All that we regard as lying at the heart of modern philosophy, at the heart of individualism, flows from this. The emphasis on the individual seeped into all aspects of culture in the western world.

Almost equally important for the development and growth of that concept of privacy at the heart of modern civilization have been the changes associated with the

Industrial Revolution. In some ways what has happened has been paradoxical. As urbanization has increased alongside an ever-expanding population, so the amount of physical space enjoyed by most individuals has declined dramatically. At the same time, the expectation of private life, of "privacy," and of what society at large would call "personal space," has developed.

This paradox is not new, of course. Society has long been familiar with the notion that privacy in a city can be greater in reality than it is in a small village. There is no necessary correlation between the concentration of habitation and the ability to limit awareness of personal details. In an urban environment people may, inevitably, live cheek-by-jowl with their neighbors while actually knowing them far less intimately. And yet what might be considered intrusion or gossip is often less common. In modern life, prurience has often been reserved for those unfortunate "celebrities" whose privacy is first invaded by telephoto lenses, then published in the pages of the tabloid media. We might well know more about their marriages than we do about that of the couple next door.

It has been this urbanization, which accompanied the Industrial Revolution, that led to the formulation—dependent of course upon the earlier evolution of the concept of the individual—of the modern notion of privacy: precisely in response to the unhealthily crowded urban environment that made it so difficult.

In 1890, a renowned study was written—a study sometimes called "the most influential law journal piece ever published"—by two lawyers called Louis Brandeis and Samuel Warren, one of whom (Brandeis) went on to become a US Supreme Court justice. The piece was entitled "The Right to Privacy" and was composed in response to technological and societal change, to what its authors referred to as "recent inventions and business methods." Rather vaguely, the authors defined this privacy as "the right to be let alone."[1]

In reaction to what they saw, aptly enough, as intrusion by journalists taking advantage of contemporary technological innovation, which made possible new invasions of privacy—in this case, the use of covert instant photography—and bearing in mind the inadequate protection provided at the time by the Fourth Amendment to the US Constitution, they argued for the addition of a new common law right that would give individuals the right to this protection. In part this was necessitated by a presumption that it was acceptable for individuals to use force, deadly if need be, to protect themselves from intrusion.[2]

This was a notable moment in what, over the last couple of centuries, has been a recurring pattern, as technology has steadily chipped away at privacy (having fashioned the notion of privacy in the first place, first through the printing press and then through the changes attendant upon the Industrial Revolution) presenting it with serious new challenges demanding serious new solutions. It has required legal protections enacted by the state to guard against threats to privacy by technology. The process is continuing now and shows no sign of coming to an end.

I've mentioned the challenges of photography, and the legal solution advanced by Brandeis and Warren. During and immediately after the Second World War—just as Galbraith was working on the ideas that he formulated in works like *The New Industrial State*—came the first photocopier, pioneered in particular by a man named Chester Carlson from the West Coast US city of Seattle.

In the early years of the Great Depression, Carlson— hunting for work—wrote letters to eighty-two companies, not one of whom offered him a job. He worked eventually in patents, where his experiences confirmed what he had noticed already: "the need for a quick, satisfactory copying machine that could be used right in the office." For such a device, he recalled, there seemed "such a crying need."

Young, recently married, and in financial need himself, "the possibility of making an invention," he thought, "might kill two birds with one stone. It would be a chance to do the world some good and also a chance to do myself some good."[3]

After early, pungent, and inflammatory experiments were banished (understandably) from his apartment kitchen by his wife, the eventual result was what we now call the photocopier. In October 1948, the first commercial machine, the Xerox Model A, was released. Cumbersome and complex by modern standards, it was itself quickly copied and improved. And while most failed in the early stages to recognize the technology's importance (IBM being only one of many companies to turn Carlson down) a few did see its potential. One observer—staggered by an invention no one had foreseen, and toward which no one else was working—wisely called the invention "the biggest thing in imaging since the coming of photography itself."[4]

Just like photography, though, the photocopy or "Xerox" posed significant questions. With a vastly increased ease of replication, replication itself grew very significantly. People do not, of course, simply copy original documents. By the mid-1980s, when photocopying was widely available, it was calculated that the average document had already been copied some thirteen times.[5] The chance of limiting access to material—which was reduced so significantly first with the invention of the printing press—has subsequently fallen much further. It is of course notorious how unsuccessful were attempts by regimes like that in Nazi Germany to eradicate published material by burning books, and that was more than a decade before the Xerox 914 was introduced in 1959.

Other technological developments likewise created significant new threats to the concept of privacy, and new challenges for the law to attempt to address. In 1967, more than half a century after Brandeis and Warren, a legal professor at Columbia University named Alan Westin published what has become a landmark book called *Privacy and Freedom*. Again, technological change had created new challenges for the law to address—new threats to the concept of privacy. In addition to the Xerox machine were things like illegal wiretapping and the pervasive and unregulated use of polygraphs (lie detectors): phenomena that Brandeis and Warren had had no reason to address. Westin was also the first to confront, in a significant way, areas like consumer data privacy, and consumer data protection.

In this book and others, Westin consolidated and advanced Brandeis and Warren's work to such an extent that he is credited now with having played a predominant role in fashioning the modern field of privacy law. He defined privacy as "the claim of individuals, groups, or institutions to determine for themselves when, how, and to what extent information about them is communicated to others."[6] He tried not to sit too clearly in one of the opposing camps, professing himself an advocate of "balance"—conscious both of the desires and interests of the large companies who often employed him and those of the "average" consumer.[7]

Then, in 1972, a commission was created in the US by Elliot Richardson—President Nixon's head of Health, Education, and Welfare. The following year this commission issued a landmark report, which included a *Code of Fair Information Practices*, or what has been called a "bill of rights for the computer age."[8] The code advocated the careful regulation of the keeping of personal data or records, urging that people must be kept informed about what data was kept and by whom, that they must be able to review and amend any data held, and that data kept for one purpose must not be used, without further authority, for another. Whether or not as a result of wartime occupation (and the attendant experience of malign government intrusion), the principles outlined in Richardson's report were actually enacted in most European countries—though they were not in the US itself.

Pandora's Inbox

Similar, significant threats to privacy came, of course, with the comparatively recent inventions of email and the internet. The ease of forwarding has seen the growth of unintended, "viral" emails—the speed of replication leading to this now-ubiquitous epidemiological metaphor. One thinks of the first "viral" email: sent by a young navy pilot in Bosnia to a group of his friends in the mid-1990s. As has so often been true since, by the time numerous high-ranking individuals (generals in this case) had been implicated in its spread, any punitive or containing measures were impossible.

So while email might just be "electronic mail," the element of privacy that largely existed with physical mail (occasional steaming open of envelopes and clandestine surveillance aside) has, crucially, disappeared. What began as a means of communication between a few close acquaintances exploded; now little can be done to alter the basic model. Pandora's inbox is open.

It is obvious to almost all of us that our emails are not always private. We notice the remarkable coincidence that an email we sent regarding holidays in Crete is followed by a proliferation of advertisements on our email account about Grecian holidays. If the same thing happened as the result of something we had sent to a friend in the mail, in a sealed envelope, it would cause us profound unease. But in the internet world it leaves us largely unbothered; we accept that this is simply part of the deal and allow algorithms access to our data.

Precisely the same thing happens, of course, with more general correspondence that we post on internet social sites. What is called "programmatic advertising"—the targeting of adverts at people with a known interest in the thing being advertised—is much more valuable to companies (and as a result much more expensive: six to eight times more) than untargeted, random adverts.

Of course, people have long known this, and to a limited extent this kind of targeting has been attempted for decades, though through content. Advertisements for cooking products or recipes predominate during cookery programs, ones for gambling during breaks in sporting coverage, and so on. But the targeting of advertising has become vastly easier and more precise now that people's apparently private correspondence is routinely scanned and its information used (Google has just ended this practice, however[9]). The more that is known about the private desires or traits of individual human beings, the more personalized and targeted such material is likely to become. This is as true with regard to advertisements for goods as it is of political advertising—bids for our vote and for our loyalty.

Precisely the same can be said of internet usage more broadly. Our internet searches are public, and they lead to us receiving online advertisements for products identical or remarkably similar to whatever it was we recently sought. Again, we know this. We are not blind to the fact that Amazon, for instance, "recommends" precisely the books at which we have been recently looking, or ones eerily similar. But we are not, perhaps, as concerned about it as we should be.

While Galbraith was hostile to an advertising industry that generated demand in a world where wants were no longer "anchored primarily in physical need"—those "intense and lachrymose voices urging highly improbable enjoyments"—companies feel the need to establish a loyalty to their brand.[10] As a population, we trust brands that we see, from their use of advertising, have invested in their reputation. But we do need to be alive to the risks, and to impose precautions.

The Internet Permafrost

In general, citizens today find it harder to escape from their past. Memory lives long on the internet. Uploaded material—photographs, writing—is frozen in a permafrost, as it were, ready to be revived and re-presented to the world whenever it is deemed suitably relevant or embarrassing. It is impossible to leave one's past behind. No wonder that campaigners advocate a "right to be forgotten." Of course, this could happen to some extent in the old world. One could publish an article, or write a letter, at twenty, the contents of which seemed regrettable at fifty. But it was much less likely to see the light of day after thirty years.

In its current form, the internet was designed to cater to a reasonably small community. As a result, the need for privacy and security did not feature highly in its original construction. Now, after an astonishingly rapid expansion has extended internet access to a large and rising percentage of the global population, it is very hard to go back and instate privacy that was not there at its inception or design.

Encryption technology does offer one significant solution for now, as quantum computing may make most forms obsolete in the future. Of course, anything that would make it harder for an eavesdropper to access communications is unpopular with law enforcement, which might thereby be shut out. It would, however, allow electronic communications to be private, or at least to aspire to privacy in the way in which written, signed, and sealed mail did. Not perfect, perhaps: sometimes encryption can be broken, just as private mail was able at times to be intercepted, steamed open, and resealed. But, in general, it was a system effective, reliable, and private enough that people grew to depend upon it: to depend upon its security as well as upon the time that delivery took.

Encryption can be an inflammatory subject. From a law enforcement perspective, there are certainly disadvantages in free societies to not being able to read every message at will. Government agencies regularly claim the right to a "back door," permitting them access to anything they should require. Many recall a high-profile instance in which the FBI demanded access to a locked iPhone while pursuing a counter-terrorism case, only for Apple to refuse to comply on principle. (The FBI did get in eventually, with the assistance of a firm from Israel.) In that case, popular sympathy probably lay more with the government agency than it did with Apple. (No useful information was gained from cracking the phone.)

In fact, though, we do need to recognize that terrorism in its current guise is a personal rather than a systemic threat: it is a grave threat to individuals, of course, and certainly not a threat we are minimizing—but at the same time not a threat to the society of which the individuals are part.

On the other hand, secret communications are certainly a fundamental threat to dictatorships. They pose a much greater risk to unfree societies than they do to free ones; and for this reason it is in the interests of all of us who do live in free societies to encourage them. I would argue that encryption is critical in fact to any successful modern society—and to a successful international community—for precisely the reason that it allows the same degree of reliance as was provided by a confidential postal service, in some countries, centuries ago.

These points have been clearly on display for more than twenty years in the US response to 9-11 and to terrorism in general, whether al-Qaeda-inspired or not. A large part of the response in America came in what is known as the Patriot Act—first signed into law by President George Bush on 26 October 2001, and many of whose clauses are scheduled to expire or "sunset" unless they are renewed.

Within this act is an infamous clause (Section 215), which allows the FBI—the government—to snoop, arguing that business records, including emails, have no expectation of privacy. The leaks made by Edward Snowden have permitted a revealing and alarming look at the way in which government has been able, beneath a cloak of secrecy, to collect phone records and monitor its population. The hidden behavior has outraged many and certainly changed the standpoint of some leading politicians. Again, the world was beset by genuine dangers; democracy had genuine enemies. It's a situation in which, again, impeccable and benign intentions have ended up posing a serious danger, in which a cautious mindset "however well-intentioned" has culminated in posing "a bigger threat to American democracy than al-Qaeda."[11]

Consider too the impact of mobile phone technology in significantly eroding our privacy while adding to our convenience. The prevalence and capabilities of mobile phones challenges to a huge extent the idea of privacy to which we are accustomed. It is barely understood by most, but for those who carry a mobile phone (and of course few in the modern world do not) there really is no privacy. Information becomes available to phone companies regarding all the movements made by the person carrying the phone, providing only that these companies have access to both the data and to sufficient computing power (they do).

This is something of which people are dimly aware but not perhaps sufficiently concerned. So far, the public has always accepted a higher level of convenience in return for lower levels of privacy or security. In most cases they are unlikely to care if some faceless person or organization can trace their movements, their internet searches, their purchases, or whatever. The sort of snooping about which people used to worry is increasingly practical for those who would. While, generations ago, it was simply not possible to eavesdrop upon millions of phone calls simultaneously due to manpower constraints, now that AI can do it instead, it becomes a viable proposition. Computers can listen to millions of calls, and they can pick out the tiny number relevant to whatever they have been programed to seek. I am confident that China is a leader in this technology.

As is obvious from my introductory remarks about the comparatively recent past, what we may be faced with now is a return to what was in many ways a longstanding norm: Privacy did not exist. For a while it did. And now it may vanish once again. Perhaps, though, provided that we are aware of the risks and are sufficiently determined, we can protect the privacy that is so profoundly threatened by the internet, the mobile phone, and much other modern technology. In 1995, Scott McNealy, the CEO of

Sun Microsystems said, "There is no privacy. Get over it." Truer words may never have been spoken.

MEDIA AND TECHNOLOGY

Media and technology are symbiotic. There is constant tension between greater markets and piracy. It was technology that created first the printing press, then the phonograph, and then motion pictures. The advent of the digital age was no less benign. New production techniques both improved quality and lowered costs. The only cloud on the horizon was the Xerox 914 (introduced in 1959), which introduced the specter of piracy for printed materials.

It was digital technology that enabled the launch of one of the most successful media formats ever: the digital compact disc, or CD—even if high prices at the time for both the media and the players made CDs seem (quite wrongly of course) as if they would be a niche format.

Today all of these turning points look minor compared to the invention of social media, initiated by Facebook in 2004.

How the Internet Became the Internet

Cheaper, faster, and smaller—in the technology industry the advances are relentless. It is a treadmill on which you have to advance just to stay still, or stay in business. When the single-chip computer was introduced in the early 1970s, few understood the implications that it would have when combined with the pace of technological advance that was enshrined in Moore's Law. Makers of other components were forced to innovate at the same pace, and so computers too became ever cheaper, ever faster, and ever smaller.

What once, therefore, were huge behemoths that occupied an entire room instead became desktops that were suitable for home use—with the Apple II, which was introduced forty years ago, or the IBM Personal Computer five years later. The invention of VisiCalc saw the Apple II transform overnight from a distinct oddity into an invaluable, almost indispensable piece of machinery. The phenomenon was then repeated on the IBM PC by Lotus 123.

In 1990, the world already had a global communication system in the Public Switched Telephone Network. A true marvel of engineering at the time, the PSTN enabled voice communication around the globe, and—in the developed world at least—connectivity was large. The network was not built for computers at all, and the technology was "circuit-switched," meaning that it enabled a direct connection between your phone and mine. Nevertheless, by 1980 there were vast computer networks built on top of the PSTN (most notably defense systems, as well as the American Airlines SABRE reservation system).

Although modems had been around for a long time, Hayes Microcomputer Products introduced the first smart modem in 1981, and it was this that made it easy for personal computers to connect. A modem, of course, is what allows computers to send data over voice telephone lines. Modems soon became cheaper, faster, and smaller—an inevitable process. Before long, thirty characters per second had become almost twenty times faster. Suddenly, personal computers could exchange data with each other and with central servers, a development exploited by AOL to huge success.

All these networks were what computer scientists call "star networks": every connection was a direct link back to a central computer site. Already, though, there were rumblings about a new form of networking, this time called "packet-switching." With its beginnings in the mid-1970s at Xerox PARC, Ethernet created the physical means to allow many computers to share a single physical network. At very much the same time, Kahn and Cerf developed the specifications for TCP/IP, the network protocol that is used today for the internet. Together with modems, these specifications unleashed what today we call the internet starting in 1993.

In the beginning, the internet had a narrow focus: no one developed it to be what it is today. Technology tends, though, just like water, to find its own level. The internet grew organically—because you could just join it. And it continued to grow. And grow. Then, once another specification, HTTP, along with Mosaic (the first genuine consumer browser) had made the internet of the early 1990s a genuine consumer network, things really began to accelerate.

Technologists like to refer to things as "stacks"—by which they mean layers of functionality. This is what makes the future so unpredictable, because adding or changing a layer affects everything else in the stack. Once the browser was launched with text pages, others quickly enhanced it so that it could handle photographs, then music and video. The internet had become a full-fledged enter-tainment network, and it has only expanded from there. In the process it has subsumed other communication and entertainment channels.

Pirates

At first the CD was a huge boon for the music industry because people bought their existing music library anew. It was almost free money. Of course, things that seem too good to be true often are, or precede a less-advantageous development. Sure enough: the PC industry decided to exploit the cheap and available hardware and media offered by the CD as a data-storage mechanism. Before long, CD drives were available, which allowed users to write their own CDs on their PC—PCs then became a vehicle for duplicating or remixing CDs. This, for the music industry, was a bad dream, one that turned into a nightmare with the launch of Napster in 1999.

Although people could share files over the internet from the beginning, doing so was cumbersome and time consuming. And, of course, they had to find the files in the first place. Napster solved these problems. People could quickly find others with music they liked and could quickly "share" their own files. The wiring of college dormitories with high-speed networking accelerated the change. The piracy of copyrighted material that ensued was a massive wake-up call to the industry.

In the shadows, yet another major development was looming, as hard disk drives—like so much else—became smaller, faster, and cheaper. Today, an average PC has hundreds of billions of characters of disk storage, compared to five megabytes when they were first introduced (a figure that then seemed large). In fact, the first tiny disks lacked a market. They found one in MP3 players. "Carry your music library with you," went the tempting invitation, though it remained a niche market until Apple launched the iPod. Over 100 million units later, the rest, of course, is history.

Even more important than the iPod was its companion software: iTunes. Most of the focus has been on Apple's ground-breaking store, offering consumers the ability to buy music one track at a time in an easy and convenient way. However, iTunes also made it easy to import your existing music, from CDs or elsewhere (especially in college dormitories), and this is what drove its early success.

At first, very little of the music on iPods was purchased from iTunes. It was easy simply to import other people's libraries, copying that was beyond the reach of policing. (The industry associations focused on file-sharing over the internet, but ineffectually even then.) Steve Jobs made a point of telling consumers not to steal music, while Apple products unquestionably facilitated it. For performers or composers, there are many opportunities to be compensated. Free music may still be valuable, as promotion for a concert tour for example. So they are less likely to mind the loss of royalties. Labels, however, did not typically share in revenues outside of recorded music, causing a widening gap between the industry and its artists—a gap accelerated by social networking.

In retrospect, the CD changed things more than was initially apparent. The virgin spin of a vinyl LP continued to be unmatched, but the wonder of digital technology like the CD is that every play sounds the same: the 1st, the 100th, the 1,000th. Music became a commodity, and nobody noticed.

Music libraries had once been a source of self-esteem, of pride. Whether LPs or CDs, people displayed them and encouraged friends to browse them. Almost overnight these libraries became passé. With your library now on your iPod, your measure of status became the number of songs on it. Individual tracks by individual artists became less important.

The movie industry, meanwhile, saw the huge boost that CDs gave to music and followed quickly with the DVD, which, until the internet, became the most rapidly adopted consumer innovation ever. (For films, of course, there was no vinyl equivalent.) The DVD brought high-quality movie viewing and listening to the home, along with additional features. Its creators avoided earlier errors and made sure that adult content was available.

The key thing, however, was that film was now available in digital form, in high quality. It too had become just bits. Having watched what happened with CDs, though, the film industry was very concerned about piracy from the beginning.

Their strategy had three main components: (1) copy protection, (2) legislation, and (3) legal downloads. The Content Scrambling System that protected DVD content was in one sense old news: securing confidential or secret information on computers was an old problem in the national security space. Here the same techniques were being applied at a massive scale for all consumers. Essentially, the content is written to the DVD in an encrypted form, and the movie industry licenses DVD player manufacturers with the key needed to decrypt the content for playback.

The movie industry also had geographic windows to protect. Given that movies are released and priced differently by geographic areas, DVDs include region-coding, limiting playback to players licensed for that region. The industry knew that no form of copy protection was fool proof. The mantra was "keep honest people honest." In the United States, a grand bargain was struck in the Digital Millennium Copyright Act, which made it illegal to circumvent copy protection but protected online service providers from liability for the actions of their customers. Similar protections were granted in the European Union in 2001.

All this effort soon came to nothing, however, because in 2002 Jon Johansen published DeCSS software, which simply removed all the copy protection. Although prosecuted, Johansen was not convicted, and the software became widely available on the internet. The Norwegian courts decided that he could not be convicted for stealing content that he owned.

The third leg of the strategy was Movielink, a legal service to permit the downloading of movies over the internet. Cumbersome and flawed from the beginning, investors sold the business at a reported cumulative loss of $150 million—at the same time Apple was able to launch and sell video downloads through iTunes.

Movie files are, not surprisingly, many times larger than music files. At the relatively slow speeds at first provided by consumer internet, downloading the files took a very long time. That was the industry's best defense against piracy, but that of course has now largely gone. The initial 512 kilobits per second of household broadband connection is now often 100 to 2,000 times higher. Size, as a defense, simply does not last. If you have more processing power available, you can also compress files—90 percent perhaps for a DVD—while losing very little (if any) quality, and this makes sharing a lot easier.

TCP/IP and Ethernet, the fundamental technologies on which the internet is based, create a network in which all actors are inherently alike, which means you can have peer-to-peer communications in which one computer on the network talks to another computer on the network. This has been there from the beginning, but it attracted little notice. In 2001, however, there was yet another layer change in the form of BitTorrent. Though technical, this is important to understand. No one thought of moving large files around when Ethernet and TCP/IP were originally designed, and both incorporate a sense of equity in making sure that the network is fairly shared. This creates an opportunity to improve download speeds by downloading not from one place but from many places. That is what BitTorrent did: allowed faster downloads in return for you agreeing to help others by letting them download from you. BitTorrent and its extensions enabled anyone to be a broadcaster on a large scale. Faster internet speeds, however, made even this redundant—a purely short-term phenomenon.

Social Media and the Attention Economy

Web 2.0 was originally the name of a conference, but it rapidly became the name for another internet phenomenon. What was Web 2.0? While there was no real definition, it seemed to connote the introduction of user-generated content as a major feature. It is not about technology, in other words, but about how that technology is used. Today, Web 2.0 seems outmoded and rather quaint. We are at the beginning of Web 3.0 and the metaverse lies just beyond.

There are now three clearly identified groups of users: "creators"—those who actually create the content, reckoned to be about 3 percent or less of all users; "curators"—the critical group who modify content, tag it (attach descriptive labels), and forward it (Jeremy Liew of Lightspeed Ventures described them as using the mouse but not the keyboard); and the rest of us who, most of the time at least, are "consumers."

Curators are the group who makes something go viral: they are the key to spreading content across a vast audience. Unpaid, they invest their time to inform their friends and to earn their respect. Far more than any other editorial source, their recommendations are trusted and believed. Engaging them, motivating them, and rewarding them is the key to success for most internet offerings. These are also the superspreaders of misinformation.

From its inception, the internet has been about communications. The biggest applications at AOL were always email and instant messaging. Instant messaging added a new feature in presence: the ability to see who else amongst your friends was online. A minor feature change allowed users to post a message that friends could quickly see. Users quickly expanded their usage of this feature to communicate more generally. Much of messaging uses similar, if less formal, "buddy lists" to forward interesting content among friends and colleagues. Very little, if anything, on social media today was not there in some (perhaps primitive) form on AOL.

Social networking began in the late 1990s, but it was probably Friendster in 2002 that first made the concept mainstream. Friendster was quickly surpassed—except in some geographic areas—by MySpace, which became a true web phenomenon.

What exact chemistry brought MySpace its initial success is elusive. Many others tried to capture it. The founders gave credit to offering pretty women in Los Angeles $20 to register. MySpace was free-spirited, with a focus on music. It gave its users great freedom of expression and great freedom in what could be posted. Above all, it became a hit early. Being on MySpace became a badge of honor, while introducing someone to MySpace was a way to build friendships. It certainly changed the nature of the relationship between bands and their fans.

Nevertheless, the great innovation in social networking was Facebook. Created by Mark Zuckerberg and some friends while he was a student at Harvard, Facebook continues to redefine what it means to be a social networking site. Coverage was originally limited to a few colleges, then to all colleges, then expanded to high schools, then to other select organizations, and then to the world. Today Facebook has over four billion members—more people than consider themselves believers in Catholicism.

From the beginning, Facebook has tried to balance access with genuineness. The exact chemistry is elusive.

An early innovation was the wall, which let your friends write public messages on your profile for all to see. But that seems irrelevant now. Facebook today is all about the news feed. If you don't use Facebook, it is probably hard to conceptualize; think of reading a newspaper and seeing a refined selection of all the things that your friends just did. Never before has it been so easy to stay in touch with such a large group. The launch of the news feed was not hailed as a major event, but it should have been.

From its college roots, Facebook has grown far. It is now the most popular social networking site in the world. It has integrated pictures and video seamlessly, along with mobile phones. It wants to be people's operating system for life: their chief source of both news and entertainment.

Social networking has changed the dynamics of media promotion completely. Viral marketing can swamp any campaign, for good or for bad, in hours. A mediocre movie is known as such by the end of the first prime-time showing. A great song from a little-known group can be a hit in days. The expression to go viral is understood nearly universally.

The original challenge for social networking sites was making money, something that is hard to believe when looking at the numbers for Facebook now. What we know

now, of course, is that targeted advertising is a very, very profitable business. Online ads are priced in terms of a cost per thousand impressions (CPM), and while untargeted ads earn very little (say, fifty cents per thousand), targeted ads easily earn ten to twenty times as much—or much more—depending on the data available. This is not a small business. Today, transactions per day are in the order of a TRILLION. The complex computing that happens each time you view an ad is mind-boggling, but it all happens in a few hundred milliseconds, a trillion times a day.

YouTube brought video clips to this party, and people loved it. Some clips are original, and some are favorite clips from favorite movies or TV shows. But the power of clips is clear. As users, we use clips (rather like we use music) as nouns by which to communicate who we are to others. We love to engage others in our likes and dislikes. Facebook and its sister site Instagram now compete across the board. New entrants Snap and TikTok, as well as WeChat from China, are all playing the same game: the attention economy.

All human beings have 168 hours to live each week. Surviving (eat, sleep) takes time. Work takes time. We are left with a certain number of hours each week (variable by week and by person) with which we can decide what to do.

Why do so many of us consume media, and if we do, which media? This is not as simple a question as it may seem. We consume media in order to learn and in order to be entertained, but we also consume media as an alternative to loneliness and boredom. Most importantly, we consume media in order to belong. At one extreme, media is a disconnected form of social networking: it creates groups into which we can self-select.

There is a dangerous flip side to this coin, however. Historically, media has acted as a social glue, making us a more connected society. Even commercials did that. Whereas in somewhere like South Korea it has long been a top priority to use media to create a sense of community, in the western world this role has eroded.

Layers of Ads

Putting ads on the internet was considered a breakthrough by many. It very rapidly became a large business. When AOL first introduced digital ads, no one really knew what they were worth—so people guessed. Initially the guesses were probably high. Page views, the act of a browser displaying a page, became the metric of choice. The value of the ad itself obviously varied, depending on the page and its location on that page. People learned that high-value pages, such as stock quotes, turned out in fact to contain low-value ads—because people on a mission simply ignored the ads.

Metrics soon evolved to cost-per-click (CPC: paid only when the viewer clicked on the ad) and cost-per-action (CPA: paid only when the viewer not only clicked, but then did something after clicking). Both of these provided the advertiser with a vastly greater assurance of value, and effective CPMs (the delivered value per impression) rose. For whatever reason, the effective CPMs from CPC and CPA were generally higher, even much higher, than the available CPM ads, so all ad networks had enormous interest in converting to CPC and CPA. Whereas the cheapest remnant ads carry CPMs as low as 25 cents (or even less), highly targeted ones can pay effective CPMs a thousand times that. This is why almost all ads are evolving into being highly targeted: very simply, that is where the money is.

The largest innovation, however, came from Google, which introduced AdWords and later AdSense. AdWords was brilliantly simple: anyone who wanted to do so could log into Google, give a credit card, and become a web advertiser. Every time a search was run on Google, Google ran a dynamic auction among the ads that matched the terms of the search, establishing which would make it the most money. AdSense then broadened this approach, allowing anyone to insert ads into their own web pages rather than simply into Google search pages. From this simple but brilliant extension was born an entire new ad layer on the internet, and Google of course has become one of the most valuable companies on Earth.

Google was not alone in realizing that money could be made from an ad network, and with its acquisition of ad.com, AOL too moved into this space—it failed. Double-Click quickly became a major supplier of web advertising, and RightMedia added the concept of dynamic auctions, which select the ads at the moment the page is viewed, further generalizing AdWords. Google bought Double-Click, and it is now the largest ad network by far.

The concept of an ad network is simple: get a premium by being the first ad dollars bought. Go in with a network of sites and try to get as much of an advertiser's budget as possible, leaving only crumbs for others. This is the upfront concept from television, expanded and general-ized to the internet.

As more and more ads are dynamically selected, there is suddenly an enormous market for real-time demographic data about the viewer. This is creating vast new markets for information. Facebook has an ad platform in which ads can be targeted based on what Facebook knows about you. Which of course is a lot. What better set of demographic data exists? What better references for a product are there than a person's friends?

Subscription services are just now gaining traction. Remember, pay television took thirty years to take off, but there is one large difference: highly targeted ads may create more than enough revenue to support even very expensive sites. Sites with compelling content, good audience demographics, and the ability to target ads tightly can often make more money from target ads than they can capture with subscriptions.

Rupert Murdoch taught us one critical thing: the economics of confirmation bias, which adds enormously to societal polarization. We all like hearing things with which we agree, and with Fox News Murdoch proved that biasing your content to what your audience believes is incredibly profitable. The result today is a plethora of outlets offering content of all flavors and opinions—for better or for worse.

The symbiosis between technology and media is certainly not over. In fact, the greatest media changes from technology may yet be ahead of us (as much as many in media may hope that they are behind us). So how much choice do consumers need or want? Research shows that consumers react negatively to too much choice because they fear making a mistake. Consumers want to find the entertainment they want, without working hard to do it. Targeting takes even more of the decision making out of their hands.

Four things seem quite clear: (1) the future will be increasingly dominated by interactive versus static content; (2) what we choose to do will be substantially influenced by what our friends and family do; (3) all advertisements will be dynamically targeted, the targeting for which will improve the greater the access the provider has to information across all media; (4) convergence means that no network or network function will exist in isolation. Convergence is inevitable. Tomorrow, we will simply assume that all of our devices are network connected. We won't generally care to which network it is connected, or how.

Even now, it matters little how content gets to consumers and the home: broadband, cable, satellite, cellular wireless, terrestrial broadcast, and others will all be there, and with the right combination (and local storage) they can be made reasonably equivalent for many. The difference between digital cable, for example, and the internet is just a difference in network protocols. All you really need is your smartphone.

In the future it will be difficult, if not impossible, to separate social networking, music, radio, TV, movies, gaming, communication and the Internet. They will meld into something new and exciting. We will probably start our evening with social networking and, in part based on its clues, select a path for the evening from a small set generated for us by merging what friends did with our own preferences. As with all predictions, it is much easier to tell what will happen than when it will happen. But we can be sure of one thing: it will.

THE NEW POLITICS

Over the last couple of decades, society has changed fundamentally in ways that no one foresaw, and the rate of change is faster now than it has ever been. The massive technological revolution, the shape of which has been outlined in the preceding chapters, is no less unstoppable than the tide was for King Canute. Attempts to arrest technological change have always been as doomed as were those of Ned Ludd. Technology has brought great and undeniable benefits, and offers great opportunities. But it also poses great challenges and even threats for the modern democratic system. The change will accelerate: that much is certain. So we need to face it and be prepared.

Using information gathered from a variety of online sources (as discussed in Chapter 12), political parties are increasingly able to target voters. Canvassing material can be quickly assembled by computer before being sent to people digitally. It can be personalized and adapted specifically to appeal to his or her known desires, prejudices, or predilections. It can be targeted carefully—tailored to an "audience of one." Most importantly, this targeting can be combined with a plea for funds. AI will make all this even better.

For the politician, this offers obvious advantages, just as it does for the commercial advertiser. Where it was logistically and financially impossible to design and print distinct campaigning material in hard copy for delivery to individual voters (even had the information about their preferences been available, which of course it wasn't to anything like the same degree) in a digital world this has now become possible. So while the leaflets pushed through our letterboxes still target a wide audience, failing to interest a large percentage of those they reach, the campaign literature we receive or will receive on our mobile phones is aimed precisely at *us*.

What are the consequences of this development? We must be wary of too many aspects of our collective experience being undermined. A society in which we exist too often as an audience of one is an atomized society, shorn of collective bonds, ceasing almost to be a society at all. Social cohesion is important for any group including nations.

The *Oxford English Dictionary* refers explicitly in its definition of this type of society to "harmonious and interactive coexistence." There is a reason why people still derive satisfaction from going to the cinema, even while the screen size of our televisions or projectors, even the surround sound, has improved enormously; it is the sense of a shared experience, even when that experience is largely internal. In a time of coronavirus-related lockdown, we have experimented with all sorts of collective activities conducted through a computer link rather than IRL (in real life). While without doubt better than nothing, this online form of interaction falls far short of the human relationships upon which a parliament, for example, usually depends. Covid-19 extended our familiarity with electronic links beyond anything we contemplated as we began 2020.

In a political context, it is our collective experience that underpins the sense of community so vital to any democratic state. It is no coincidence that throughout history societies governed autocratically have been able to be massively diverse in terms of the identity of their population. Territories need not even be contiguous. For medieval dynastic states, for instance, it was not unusual for subjects to have little in common beyond their ultimate ruler, and for the state itself—almost any historical atlas will furnish examples—to constitute a patchwork presence rather than an unbroken block on a map. With the population exercising very little choice about their government or its activity—with no element of popular consent—it was not and is not critical that there be any shared sense of belonging to a wider family. Resistance, in these contexts, is isolated and forcefully put down. Thus of course did empires—"prisons of nations" as the Austro-Hungarian was known—manage to govern an extremely diverse population.

Only the emergence of the nation-state (in Western Europe, North America, and some other places) created the community cohesion—the sense of shared identity—that enabled the emergence of a democratic society. The results of elections needed to be respected, and subsequent government decisions likewise. As this kind of government gradually claimed a dramatically increased role in terms of redistributing wealth and providing a "safety-net" for all in terms of healthcare and social security, it became vital that members of that society sufficiently identify with one another to accept this redistribution.

Numerous attempts to create functioning democratic communities where they did not exist (in the aftermath of military interventions such as took place, for instance, in

Iraq or Afghanistan, or as the project for a European Union attempts over a broader area) have found that it is by no means easy to inculcate this communal sense in a population that does not feel it. In the contemporary world this difficulty may increase as technology threatens to undermine it (even if some significant factors, like translation technology, tend to make mutual identification between national groups easier).

What then might the impact of technological change be upon the creation or maintenance of the cohesive communities upon which democracies depend? It is now possible for political parties to canvass narrowly, to target individual voters very precisely according to their tastes and views—to "micro-target." One unfortunate ramification of this trend is likely to be that extremist views are fostered in new ways.

A broadcast, by its nature, tended to moderate extremes by the simple fact that an attempt was made—precisely as the word implies—to appeal to the broadest number of people. It made no sense in such a production to pander to views not shared by the majority: you might appeal to one while alienating one hundred. In a world in which material can be targeted individually, however, this moderating effect has ceased to apply. When benefit is anticipated from pandering to prejudice, then this is what is likely to occur—you can appeal to one without alienating anybody else. Extremes will become more populated, as well as more extreme. Instead of speaking to the middle, politicians (and people more generally) will be able to speak to the sides, safe in the knowledge that the middle will not hear.

Since nobody will be listening to all output and drawing attention to inconsistency, there will not be any need to be consistent. As movement to the extremes intensifies, polarization and bitter, unmoving gridlock (which we see politically in the US, and saw during the Brexit referendum in the UK) will become more common, as compromise and common ground become progressively harder to find.

This growing extremism, it is important to understand, is not simply a question of persuading people to cast a democratic vote for someone who is inclined to an extreme position. There have been instances in history—Adolf Hitler was one—in which someone has been democratically elected who has turned out to hold very extreme views, and who proved capable of dismantling or circumventing the restraints relied upon to uphold democratic rules. This, however, is certainly not the most likely scenario. Much more often, the result of a democratic election is more critically influenced by voter turnout.

In mature democracies, parties are likely to have a faithful body of support, for whom it would be almost unimaginable to transfer their vote to another, and certainly not to the principal competing party. What they are much more likely to do, however, is to fail to vote at all. Given that most elections in the democratic world are won on between a 50 percent and a 70 percent turnout, electoral strategists have long since worked out the immense importance of who stays home.

A decisive election result is more likely to occur after the collapse of one party's once-reliable vote than it is after a substantial rise in a rival's. So, for instance, in the electoral system in the UK—Boris Johnson's resounding victory in the general election of 2019 was more the result of a collapse in traditional Labour support among voters, who felt unable to vote for Jeremy Corbyn (without, certainly, going so far as to vote for Johnson's Conservatives), than it was of any strong upsurge in support for Johnson.

The same tendency was seen in terms of doubts cast about Hillary Clinton by social media advertisements promoted (and paid for—though not openly) by the campaign of Donald Trump. The campaign did not expect a potential Clinton voter to transfer his or her vote to Trump (a transfer that was highly unlikely); the hope was to create enough doubt to stop the vote for Clinton being cast. Reminders that Hillary Clinton–supported three-strikes-and-you're-out laws in the 1990s were very effective in reducing enthusiasm in the Black community to vote in the expected number for Clinton. It is differential turnout that wins elections: ensuring that your vote does turn out while that of the opposing side does not. This is the context in which we should view the potential impact of "narrowcasting"—its ability to increase the efficacy with which seeds of doubt are sown.

Technology has had another unwanted consequence in the US with the "Stop the Steal" claims of former president Trump and his supporters. Stoked by fears of foreign intervention in US elections and then accelerated even more by the Covid-19 pandemic, US states made enormous changes to their electoral systems to adapt. They worked. An election was held with record turnout. By the rules and process in place, Joe Biden was the winner. There can be no doubt of that.

However, the margin of victory was tiny: 42,000 votes in the right places would have changed the outcome—that's out of roughly 155 million total votes cast. The president is elected by a weighted vote of the states plus the District of Columbia. Shifting 42,000 votes would have re-elected

Trump as president. It can be no surprise that in an election decided by so few votes, there would be claims of fraud.

Usually, claims of fraud are easily disproved. In this election, however, some claims were not able to be either proved or disproved. Technology had created single points of failure such as the software in voting machines, or algorithmic signature verification on mail-in ballots. One state, Georgia, saved all the original paper and was able to prove no fraud, but in some other states this was not possible—so the claims persist. Being able to disprove fraud is important for democratic elections. Computer scientists call this non-repudiation.

In many ways this is similar to a Russian warfare technique: effectively poisoning the well, making everything look bad so that everybody distrusts everybody. Look, for example, at their strategy in the aftermath of the poisoning of Sergei Skripal and his daughter Yulia in Salisbury. Around thirty different stories of what happened were put forward by a Kremlin-sponsored media organization. The Brits did it. The Swedes did it. Yulia Skripal did it herself. Sergei's mother-in-law did it. The whole story was a fake. One story said the Russians did it—but only as a single possibility on a long list of ridiculous possibilities. The thinking is not that a listener will believe any one of them;

it is that he or she will disbelieve them all, including of course the one that says that it was the Russians who did it. Again, you don't vote for Clinton or Trump: you stay home and vote for neither.

This has all been forcefully illustrated by the current Covid-19 pandemic. Some people go to the extremes of conspiracy theory. These people are disproportionately likely to make a loud noise, are increasingly able to do so, and can exist in reinforcing bubbles of the like-minded— they can isolate themselves, to use an appropriate image (or perhaps an inappropriate one), from the restraining effect of integration in broader society.

To some extent, of course, all of this has happened before. Extreme viewpoints are scarcely new. People have long read only the newspapers or other publications that reflect their own political beliefs: it is flattering to have your own views shouted, more eloquently perhaps, back at you. (In the UK, Brits make a lot of presumptions once they know that a person is a regular reader either of the *Guardian* or of the *Daily Telegraph*, and few read both unless their job requires it.)

Now there are an exponentially increasing number of viewpoints available, and most people continue to reinforce their own with those that are similar. All evidence from social media suggests, for instance, that in the US, Democrat voters read overwhelmingly the writing of other Democrat voters, while Republicans similarly stick to their own clan. Far from being undermined, the barricade between the two is thereby cemented.

Sometimes, of course, what begins as an extreme and minority view may over time become less minority—it may even become widely accepted. (One thinks immediately of scientific ideas like Darwin's about evolution and the wide-spread disbelief and hostility it initially faced.) The fact that many now-mainstream ideas began life on the fringe provides succor to radical ideologues everywhere. The fact that many more either remain on the fringe or die out alto-gether is forgotten.

In a sense, the narrowcast is on what the entire model of a platform like Facebook is built: people sharing news and photographs and opinions with others with whom they are personally familiar, and to whom they think the mate-rial is likely to appeal.

The Wild West

In the past, social media has functioned rather as the lawless world of the wild west, without liability, without governmental authority, and with the hosting sites refusing to accept responsibility for material published there (the reader will recall Section 230 of the Communications Decency Act from Chapter 2). Facebook, for example, depends on an algorithm to decide which messages are accorded prominence and promotion. It refuses to accept liability for these algorithmic decisions. But it should. It is the creator of the algorithm, after all. "An algorithm," as has been observed, "is only as good as the assumptions you put into it."[1] The published content reflects Facebook's assumptions. The company has effectively decided which messages to promote; the denial that such a site is, in effect, a *publisher*, is simply not plausible.

Alongside the wild west, one thinks of the world of print publishing in an earlier world, in England during the seventeenth century. This was a time when regulation and punishment, both of writers and of publishers, was often extremely severe—much more so than it is in democratic countries today. No concept of a right to "free speech" yet existed. In an attempt to regulate, an "imprint" was required to provide the publisher's name, location, and the date of publication on every copy. Then, as now, what seemed to matter was disclosure. Participation needed to be identifiable. A clear trail had to link material to its ultimate source.

At the time, of course, this rule was frequently ignored—for reasons with which we might well now sympathize. Publications were issued in a clandestine manner, using fictitious imprints, or simply with bland, fake statements like "Printed by The Stationers." (The Stationers' Company was the livery company that oversaw the publishing industry.) Arguably it was rather harder to trace an anonymous author in the real world of seventeenth-century England than it is in the virtual world of the twenty-first, when most computers are usually traceable for anyone sufficiently interested in doing so.

Much as this parallel holds true in many respects, the boot is now being worn on the other foot. We should be skeptical of anyone (or anything) anonymously participating in a debate that cannot be easily traced to its participants. Social media—cyberspace generally—is a world that powerful organizations can populate with "bots": automated, computerized entities that are increasingly able to appear much like humans. This is a world in which anonymous participation should be distrusted, and regarded more often than not as propaganda. The cloak of anonymity that seemed justifiable in mid-seventeenth-century England seems now—at least in what might be called the "free world"—to be masking a guilty secret.

THE NEW
TECHNOLOGY STATE

We are living in a New Technology State: an existence in which arguably everything is or soon will be infused with technology. This book has explored how the world in which everyone lives has been very significantly influenced by present technology.

As Galbraith emphasized, "change" is no less omnipresent than "the law of economic life." What alters dramatically is not so much the *fact* of change but its *rate*. All technological change inevitably follows an S curve, with a period of relative stability preceding a very rapid and widespread transformation. As changes pile on top of one another, as change begets further change, these S curves too pile up.

Galbraith first published *The New Industrial State* in

1967, basing it on a series of Reith Lectures he had given at the BBC (as well as upon his own earlier and more famous, if less developed, work *The Affluent Society*). He looked at the shape of the modern economy, and at the ways in which it was actually very different from the classical economic models with which people like him had become familiar as students. He himself considered *The New Industrial State* to be one of his most important works, and considered the preceding decades—which he had himself experienced—to have been a time of bewildering change.

"The innovations and alterations in economic life in this century," he wrote, "and more especially since the beginning of World War II, have, by any calculation, been great." It was the role of this change, he argued—how it happened and, most importantly perhaps, the response that it engendered—that lay at the very heart of modern economic discussion. This is a sentiment that I echo, loudly and without hesitation, with regard to our own time. In retrospect, humanity has never seen anything like the change the last four decades have brought.

Of course, "progress" in the sense of economic and technological growth, has not been steady—not in our day and not in Galbraith's. The Great Recession of 2007–2009 looms large in our rearview mirror, just as the Great

Depression, which came to an end sometime in the late 1930s, did in his. It remains to be seen how large and how enduring is the damage to the global economy caused by the Covid-19 pandemic of 2020, but it is difficult to imagine that it will not be substantial.

Nevertheless, in the course of the last couple of decades, the arrival of the internet in particular has transformed our economic landscape almost beyond recognition. If all technological change forms an S curve, then the turning on of the internet was unquestionably a seismic moment. When that happened, society rapidly accelerated, past the gentle plateau—past the knee of the curve—and entered a steep climb. The speed of transformation today is greater than it has ever been. That giant leap prompted, or at least hastened, a myriad of others: in cloud computing, in artificial intelligence, in robotics, or in block chain, to name only a few.

This has been called a "new industrial revolution," but actually—hugely significant as the first Industrial Revolution unquestionably was—the label almost undersells it. For this change is unprecedented; it is not merely a sequel. Nevertheless, there is much about the scale of the contemporary economic transformation that accurately reflects what Galbraith had seen in earlier shifts.

People who grew up in the old world, the world before the internet, feel rather like William Makepeace Thackeray when he wrote about a time before the nineteenth-century appearance of the steam train: "We who lived before the railways and survive the ancient world are like Father Noah and his family out of the Ark." Suddenly, the world was transformed—it was linked in a way that was entirely unprecedented—and it could never go back. "'Tell us, grandpapa, about the old world,'" children will say, with uncomprehending astonishment, to an ever-smaller number of our ancient generation.[1]

While Galbraith might be surprised by the nature of some of the specific changes—as would we all be to see a world decades after our own time—he would scarcely be surprised by the fact that things have changed. No doubt it seemed at the time—in the 1960s—that General Motors, or General Electric, were immutable fixtures of the economic landscape (just as we might think of Amazon, or Google, or Meta today). But, as Galbraith saw, this was merely a delusion, and one that tended to suppress informed speculation about what the future might hold: "one does not wonder where one is going if one is already there."

Pace Francis Fukuyama and his famous postulation that liberal capitalism amounted to an "end of history,"

Galbraith would have found it strange, and implausible, to believe that post-war capitalism had attained any sort of perfect, terminal state.[2] Change, on the contrary, was sure to continue.

Back to the Future

There are two comparisons worth making with the past rather than with the future (for all that it might be a foreign country, the past is one at least that can be known with some accuracy):

The first is with Galbraith's own early life. He was born in Canada toward the end of 1908, meaning that he was a young adult during the 1930s. He knew and worked with people like John Maynard Keynes and Franklin Delano Roosevelt: people closely associated, invariably, with that period of human history—in the United States of America and therefore in the wider world. Galbraith's most renowned works of economic theory—including *The New Industrial State*—were published soon after the Second World War, during the 1950s and 1960s. As a young man, in other words, Galbraith lived through a period of profound economic and political change. He turned ten a matter of weeks before the end of World War I. As an adult, he experienced the extraordinary decades of the 1930s and 1940s.

Between the end of World War I and the outbreak of World War II, something like 70 percent of all jobs in the developed world changed as agriculture mechanized and the numbers of people employed on farms fell precipitously, even as the scale of these farms grew considerably. The use of animals for labor gave way to the use of the tractor and other machines. The percentage of the overall human population living and working in rural, agricultural areas fell dramatically. A much higher number moved to live and work in towns or cities.

Between 1905 and 1920—the period of Galbraith's young childhood—the number of tractor manufacturers in the US leapt from only 6 to over 160. In subsequent years it climbed higher still. Hundreds of thousands of tractors, becoming lighter, stronger, and more affordable with every year that passed, ploughed, planted, or harvested on American and European farms. The number of hours of human labor needed to produce a given weight of any crop plummeted.

In some parts even of the developed world, this transformation came a decade or two later. You might find people working in agriculture during the 1940s, say, who were still essentially pre-industrial peasants. If they were young then, they might have lived to see the arrival of the internet in their old age: an extraordinary transformation for a single generation to experience.

This earlier, interwar world was one with which Galbraith was closely familiar. He came from a farming background. His own father was a farmer in Canada as well as a school teacher. Galbraith graduated initially with a bachelor of science in agriculture from Ontario Agricultural College, and majored in animal husbandry. His first public job—after he had moved to the US and adopted American citizenship—was in the US Department of Agriculture.

This was a time when countless traditional jobs—many of which, of course, were in agriculture—were lost. "Machines," as Galbraith himself remarked in *The New Industrial State*, "have replaced crude manpower."[3] This was a time when people found themselves either forced to retrain completely and to move away from work on the land, or (more likely perhaps, particularly for those who were older) simply unable to find alternative employment, at least until the coming of World War II. The contraction of the economy in the aftermath of the Wall Street crash and the subsequent global depression made the search for alternative work all the harder.

As president of the US, Franklin Delano Roosevelt is most closely associated, certainly, with the New Deal, which enabled America to confront the Great Depression—but he did this in ways that had significant costs. Everyone over the age of sixty-five, for instance, was encouraged to retire (this was a much smaller demographic at the time). This cut the workforce, which certainly helped to address unemployment. But of course it was also very expensive. Today—in a world where the age balance of the population is very different to that of the 1930s, and many industrial countries have more elderly than young people—it would involve taxation that would be confiscatory and politically impossible.

In the modern age, the change we face is on at least the same scale as it was when Galbraith was a young man. Without doubt, a vast number of jobs with which we are familiar will be lost. To cite just one example, at present there are some 3.5 million long-haul truck drivers in the US. As the long-haul trucking industry turns to self-driving vehicles (as it is sure to do) these jobs will disappear entirely. While for some there will be other jobs in the haulage industry, there certainly won't be anything like so many of them. Many drivers will simply be laid off. On the other hand, employers currently cannot fill these positions because people are not attracted to them.

What this example illustrates—and what is generally true—is that those most affected by economic transformation will be the unknown masses. As a general rule, the jobs held by individuals whose names we neither know nor can easily find out are by far the most likely to be mechanized, and so lost. Retraining will be fundamental. This will be much easier, of course, for those who are younger and earlier in their careers. For a truck driver in his or her fifties, pursuing a new line of work will be very difficult.

The second parallel goes back in time much further, to the Industrial Revolution itself, since it is with this that a comparison with the far-reaching change facing society today is sometimes drawn.

One point needs emphasizing immediately. What is seen generally as "progress"—and which of course, economically speaking, was exactly that—was far from positive for many individuals. For them, the changes constituted a profound and altogether lamentable disruption of traditional patterns of life and behavior. The smashing of automated cotton looms during the Napoleonic Wars was simply part of a more protracted culture of violent protest against the loss of traditional jobs to machinery, which led in Britain to acts of Parliament like that of 1788 for the Protection of Stocking Frames.

In a fictional context, one thinks of the animosity portrayed by George Eliot (or Mary Ann Evans, since she no longer needs to pretend to be male) in *Middlemarch* toward the coming of the railway. The unstoppable march of modernity this might be—and the development today of driverless trucks looks much the same—but for many individual human beings this process of change is extremely painful. The young might be able to adapt; those older and either stuck in a vanishing profession or too accustomed to a suddenly outmoded practice are likely to find it much harder. From handloom weavers to coal miners to (one imagines) lorry drivers, the list of examples—and their angry and embittered, if ultimately futile, reaction to change—is very long.

It is the need to deal with this very high rate of dissatisfaction among a largely conservative population that has made the ability to mass produce drugs like alcohol (and, increasingly, others too) so important. We return to where we began in the Introduction, to the most vital invention of the Industrial Revolution: the gin still. When we think of gin in the eighteenth century, we think probably of Hogarth's print of "gin lane," of the "damned cup," which "madness to the heart conveys." We think of people incapable of feeding their children—let alone of operating heavy machinery. But without the gin still, Britain could not have experienced the Industrial Revolution at all. Beer might have been, as Hogarth also put it, a "balmy juice" and the "happy produce of our isle," but you simply couldn't brew enough of it to get everybody drunk who wanted to get drunk. Without this drunkenness, the speed and extent of change would have led to massive social unrest and, ultimately, to collapse.

Location, Location, Location

In change then, just as in change now, there is no doubting the role of simple good fortune as well as of intelligent prediction. Those who owned acres of impractical, marshy land near Westminster in London (districts like Mayfair and Pimlico) found the value of their assets rocketing with urbanization and the expansion of the capital city. One thinks, for instance, of the famously wealthy Duke of Westminster and the value of his landholding. Compare this with the often larger estates claimed by owners in Norfolk, say—much better agricultural land, but suddenly worth only the tiniest fraction of what real estate in central London is worth.

The same kind of sudden and largely unpredictable transformation still occurs today. Think of the Indian farmers of the guar bean—grown in Rajasthan as a dietary staple for centuries—whose water-absorptive properties make it suddenly in high demand, in a way that was wholly unpredicted: in the fracking industry, based many thousands of miles from the bean plantations. It has meant a soaring value for the beans (the "bean bubble"), which is closely tied, not surprisingly, to oil prices.

Or take the Ethiopian teff farmers. Teff is a grain used to make pancakes and bread. Naturally gluten-free, it looks set to capitalize on the dramatic rise in global demand for gluten-free baking products. Again, this transformation was in no way predicted; it is in fact being resisted in many quarters by those reluctant to see the same sharp rise in prices that made quinoa hard for the populations of South American countries like Peru and Bolivia to afford, despite it having long been a traditional dietary staple. There is no disputing at times that simple, unforeseen good fortune—and, of course, misfortune—plays a very significant role in who wins and who loses when change is afoot.

Alongside the violence and instability inherent in all societies, industrialization has also engendered international warfare and unprecedented environmental dilapidation. Rapid change and disruption have created violent animosities. There have been major winners and major losers, and intense competition for resources that were once scarcely valued. Simultaneously, the changes associated with industrialization have admitted a degree of destruction that was not previously imaginable. The sheer scale of the possible damage, furthermore, has involved an increasingly large percentage of the population.

No longer are we talking (as in the pre-industrial age) about a limited battlefield populated only by soldiers and their associated entourage. From at least the US Civil War—and worsening, of course, as time passed—killing, like other crafts, has been conducted on an industrial, not artisanal scale. At an extreme level, the citywide destruction seen at Hiroshima and elsewhere throughout the twentieth century has meant that an entire nation is now truly at war in a way that was not formerly so—and the horrific scale of destruction seen at Hiroshima was relatively small in comparison with the devastation that nuclear weapons might inflict today.

CONCLUSION: WHERE DO WE GO NOW?

Economists often talk about production functions: turning capital and labor into product. But countless volumes have explored this subject while saying little or nothing—quite wrongly—about the role played by technology. It is critical to understand that production functions are not static. Information is a major factor of production, and as technology has rapidly improved, information has become dramatically cheaper, as well as easier and quicker to access. The simple world of capital and labor—that of Marx and Engels, as well as countless others—is now gone. Labor is not a single market anymore, a competitive supply of a single type. Talent is the new input, and the relevant talent is concentrated in a tiny number of people.

Unloved (except by economists, of course) production functions are the bedrock of neoclassical capitalism. They reflect the world at the time of capitalism's creation as a doctrine. But times have changed. Capital may be fungible—that is, interchangeable—but people are not. The very essence of modern business is information, and every function reflects technology, which continues to change at incredible speed. As soon as you incorporate these factors, as you certainly must, almost all of the policy prescriptions go wrong.

Looking back, the history of computing has consisted of a succession of eras, each lasting about a decade, each leaving its own stamp on economic reality. In the first generations, the mechanics of the machine were crafted to the output required. That didn't last. Long ago, software allowed general-purpose computing to replace special-purpose computing. The exponential growth correctly foretold by Moore's Law has driven and underpinned these changes, rendering possible the computer's massive expansion in capability. After all this time, the improvement may just now be slowing. Certainly some scientists have doubted, in the last decade, that it is continuing or indeed that it can continue. But of course these doubts have existed before.

The impact of computers really took off once there was a single dominant player: IBM, International Business Machines, as the "Computing-Tabulating-Recording

Company" had become known in 1924. By themselves, computers are only useless consumers of energy. In order to be useful they need software, and no one company could ever write all of the software that is required. The path to having the most software, however, is for everyone to write to the same standards, and this leads to increasing returns to scale, which—to its credit—neoclassical economics recognizes as leading to market failure.

Capitalism vs. Competition

Metcalfe's Law, as we saw in Chapter 9, states that the value of any network is proportional to the square of the number of people who are connected to it, as the number of possible connections grows exponentially. This is fundamental to modern life. Facebook, LinkedIn, WeChat, Instagram, WhatsApp, SnapChat, Tencent, TikTok, and Twitter all dominate in their spaces because of this dependency circle: the more members you have as a social network, the more people want to join.

This domination, though, means an effective monopoly. And thus the history of the computing industry is a succession of antitrust cases. All of which, it should be said, have been largely ineffective. The history is not one of competition, but of a succession of dominant firms, each giving way only as new paradigms emerge. Mainframe computers to minicomputers to workstations to PCs to networks to devices. All of this has been driven by Moore's Law, by the accompanying decline (also caused by Moore's Law) of the costs of moving data, and by software. We are now starting a new round of antitrust actions in both the United States and the European Union.

All of this means that the world we live in resembles not at all the world of Ricardo and Smith. There are a trillion programmatic advertising events per day on the internet, as corporations optimize the messages that they pay to deliver to us. The data they have on us is enormous, as are the computer resources used to process it. It is certainly not perfect competition.

The mindset of Silicon Valley is reflected by Peter Thiel, one of the great venture capitalists of this era: the goal of any entrepreneur is to create a monopoly to generate profits. Of course, it is. Whatever some might think about competition, this is the essence of capitalism.

On the hardware side, the supply of the chips has become ever more concentrated: into a handful of manufacturers, primarily based in Taiwan. Semiconductor fabs are very, very expensive. They only make sense economically when the semiconductors are produced in incredible volumes. So there are only a few of them, concentrating risk.

The software side is dominated by a core group of individuals blessed with exceptional talent. Traditionally, this group was thought to be about 10,000 strong, and IBM in the 1980s, Microsoft in the 1990s, and Google in the 2000s all claimed to employ at least half of this global pool. The pool is probably bigger today, but the proportion employed by Google, Apple, Microsoft, Facebook, and Tencent is still extremely high.

This dominance is only natural. These firms can and do pay much larger salaries, and they offer more exciting, rewarding work performed with colleagues who share similar passions and abilities. As they accumulate more of these exceptionally able people, the internal productivity of these firms goes up, while the ability of others to compete goes down. Software is a stack, and as with any stack, control of the bottom layer is critical. Winning firms get others to invest in creating software that runs on their stack. Which in turn generates values that they can tax.

This, in a nutshell, is the debate over the Apple App-Store. Apple has a beautiful platform with over a billion users. A key attraction of this platform is the vast ecosystem of apps available from third parties through the Apple AppStore. There is no way to get an app onto your device other than through this AppStore. If you build an app, Apple takes a 30 percent cut if you charge money, at least for the first year. You have to submit your apps for inspection, and only Apple can then release them—to your customers. Governments are already challenging this situation, starting with the Netherlands and South Korea.

There is an opaque review process (defended by Apple as protecting its users, though many third parties complain that the company uses it to tilt the playing field toward Apple). Apple has historically refused to allow you to offer a store within an app that competes with any other store offered separately by Apple. Indeed, Apple never told anyone anything different. But to some app vendors, these rules are unfair, and recent court decisions have not gone entirely Apple's way.

Technology has historically undermined the economic power it creates. IBM and Microsoft are the most obvious examples, but there are more (consider the short leap from CD to Napster). IBM is still living off its past and fumbling the future. Microsoft under a new CEO has reinvented itself for the new order. This time may be different. We are near the asymptote of this technology curve. It is hard to see what displaces the huge installed base that exists today. Artificial intelligence, metaverse, quantum computing— these will play an important part in our future, but I am not sure they create a discontinuity; the current tech giants are the leaders in these technologies across the board.

Time to Pony Up

The technology giants benefit enormously from two factors. First, they have been able to largely monopolize the market for top technology talent by being able to offer above-market but below-value compensation others cannot match, with the exception of potential startup unicorns. The vehicle for this has been equity-based compensation, aided and abetted by favorable tax treatment and short-term focused equity markets. Second, their key raw material is aggregated personally identifiable information, which they collect by offering free services. Again, the free services are above-market but below-value, as there is little value in one person's data but enormous wealth in the aggregated data of millions. Just as we tax oil companies on the oil extract from the Earth, we may need to tax aggregated personally identifiable information (PII).

There is a virtuous circle here—for the companies in

question. Top talent yields good business results yields rising stock price yields tax advantages and high compensation. To level the playing field, here are six possible policy options:

1. ***Excise Tax on Corporate Market Value:*** A straw man for this would be 1 percent on value over $100 billion rising by 1 percent for each incremental $100 billion. Thus, a corporation valued at $300 billion would pay $3 billion in tax. Robustness in the economy is a public good properly regulated by the government. This tax simply reflects the principle that diversity is good and increases robustness, but it lets the market decide how and why to divide. Competition is good for society and the economy. This is as likely to boost shareholder value as reduce it. This is market-based antitrust policy.

2. ***Excise Tax on PII:*** Personally identifiable information is the core value for the tech giants, more so than technology. We need to tax tech giants on the PII they collect. Individual value is low; aggregated value is high. Charging for personal use is not realistic. The tax should be targeted to collect, say, 15 percent of all revenue derived from aggregated PII.

3. *Excise Tax on Stock Trades:* As mentioned in Chapter 7, this is called a Tobin tax after its initial developer, James Tobin. Essentially, it says modern capitalism is too efficient and overweights the present. This offsets this. It is a low tax, maybe 0.5 percent, but it would help refocus the market on economic rather than trading value, and it reduces the ability of management to spike stock prices. Wall Street traders oppose this, but society gains in the long term.

4. *Excise Tax on Tax Advantaged Income:* Tax advantaged income (TAI) would include all income taxed at capital gains rate as well as consumption financed by net loans received and not invested. An excise tax of 10 percent would be due on all TAI in excess of $5 million plus an additional 10 percent on all TAI over $50 million and a further 10 percent on all TAI over $500 million. This retains tax incentives but reduces them at high levels.

5. *Excise Tax on Stock Repurchases:* Stock repurchases increase executive pay, which is tied to stock price. It is not a surprise that corporate management favors it. There are some more legitimate reasons, so the tax might be relatively low, say 5 percent. The US Inflation Reduction Act (2022) started down this path.

6. *Flipped Tax Treatment for Equity Awards:* Tax equity compensation (like carried interest) at capital gains rates, but allow corporations to deduct only the accounting cost of these awards rather than their actual gain. This would eliminate a huge tax advantage for the tech giants, as they can currently deduct billions of a non-cash expense against their taxes but not show it in their reported results. The minimum tax on book income recently enacted in the United States and agreed worldwide is a step in this direction if it comes to pass.

Legal constraints like antitrust and regulation make billions for lawyers (which is why they like them) but they just don't work. Taxes do. We have what we have because people optimize within the rules they are given. Facebook and others did no wrong. They did what our laws and courts require them to do: maximize profits. Maybe they made business judgments that were short-term biased, but our entire capital market is focused that way. *If we want a different outcome, we must set different rules.* These are but a start, and political reality may be that none or only some are feasible. Lawyers love making themselves more important and necessary, but that is not the answer here.

Still, even these measures are not sufficient. We have

to enable anyone with the right skills to be able to excel with those skills. The US Defense Education Act may be a model. It is certainly a precedent. We need every person with the potential to be a technology performer to have that opportunity. This may require intervention all the way down to preschool. More research is needed. Only by increasing and broadening supply will we achieve the balance we want and need in our society.

Checks in the Mail

There is one other essential reform to consider. It may seem tangential or even orthogonal, but it is not: postmarked electronic communications. This requires a set of policies:

1. The national postal authority provides the ability to postmark electronic communications for a modest fee— say 10 cents or pence for email and 2 cents or pence for messages.
2. Every electronic messaging system with more than one million users would be required to support the sending and receipt of postmarked messages.
3. Each such system would be required to allow users to block non-postmarked communications outside of a

personal whitelist. This would be totally optional, but the bulk of users are likely to do so. As is true today for first-class mail, it would be illegal to obstruct or destroy a postmarked communication.

4. Where lawmakers have the right to free postal mail to communicate with their constituents, they would retain that right electronically.

Without infringing on free speech, this would immediately make it much more expensive to profit from hate and fear. The challenge, of course, is that it requires legislators to act in the public interest rather than their own. The win for society is massive. The ability of email and messaging to spread division and hate would be greatly reduced.

There are two follow-up advantages from this proposal: It creates a path to eventually end physical mail delivery by creating a replacement for first-class postal mail. The postmark would prevent non-repudiation so that the sender could prove dispatch and the recipient could verify the message. This creates a pathway to secure email voting, which in turn raises participation in democratic elections and returns some of the power to the people. What is the role of the nation-state in a world in which countries post "ambassadors" to Google? Ambassadors who are almost incontestably more critical than those to most other nations. To what will this lead?

There is nothing anyone can do to unfuck society instantly. These steps together, however, will put us back on a path to sanity.

ACKNOWLEDGMENTS

I'd like to thank Tom's family for allowing us to develop the framework for this book in peace in Florence. Thanks also to Scott Johnson for keeping us on track and organized, James Evans for helping to put flesh around the skeleton, and Christopher Gronow for creating the graphics used to illuminate Halstead Length. Alex Salkever and Richard Rippe read early drafts and provided many useful comments but share no responsibility for what followed.

Like any book, the manuscript is just the beginning, and I thank the entire team at Amplify Publishing for their help in making that transition, especially Naren Aryal, its CEO; Brandon Coward, the project manager; and Zack Gresham, the editor.

ENDNOTES

Introduction

David D. Lowman, *Magic* (Athena Press, 2000), 40.

Chapter 2

Elle Hunt, "Tay, Microsoft's AI Chatbot, Gets a Crash Course in Racism from Twitter," *Guardian*, March 24, 2016, https://www.theguardian.com/technology/2016/mar/24/tay-microsofts-ai-chatbot-gets-a-crash-course-in-racism-from-twitter?CMP=twt_a-technology_b-gdntech.

Chapter 4

John Kay, "Evolution Is the Real Hidden Hand in Business," johnkay.com, September 30, 2009, https://www.johnkay.com/2009/09/30/evolution-is-the-real-hidden-hand-in-business/.

2   Reuven Brenner, "Our Muddles Masses," First Things, January 2010, https://www.firstthings.com/article/2010/01/our-muddled-masses.

3   Ed Smith, *Luck* (London: Bloomsbury, 2012), 223; one of the winners of the 2020 Nobel Prize for Physics, Sir Roger Penrose, commented upon how slow and methodical he had always been at mathematics as a child: "I just was slow, and I'm slow at writing," he said. Obviously, this did not stop his thought—slow as it might be—from being profound. See https:// www. bbc.co.uk/news/science-environment-54420240.

Chapter 6

1   William J. Raduchel, "Managing Software Development," *Software Engineering Notes* (Association for Computing Machinery's Special Interest Group on Software Engineering) 3, no. 4 (October 1978): 22.

2   Charles Wessner and Dale Jorgenson, eds., *Measuring and Sustaining the New Economy* (Washington, DC: National Academy Press, 2002).

Chapter 8

1   This is not, of course, a law in any scientific sense. A decade later, Moore relaxed his estimate by half. Either

way, he is not disproved should it cease to operate. In 2015, he commented that what he had done was simply to make a "wild extrapolation" based upon what he saw. He has, nevertheless, continued to be right for what even he would have considered an extraordinary length of time.

2   John Kenneth Galbraith, *The New Industrial State* (first published by Houghton Mifflin, 1967).

3   Galbraith, *The New Industrial State*.

4   Ibid.

5   The average cost per launch was about $1.2 billion (in 2010 dollars) during the shuttle's operational years between 1982 and 2010. But it rises to $1.5 billion per flight when factoring in the lifetime cost of the program, according to an analysis that covered the 131 shuttle missions flown between 1982 and 2010; Jeremy Hsu, "Total Cost of NASA's Space Shuttle Program: Nearly $200 Billion," space.com, April 11, 2011, https://www.space.com/11358-nasa-space-shuttle-program-cost-30-years.html.

Chapter 9

1   The original article was published in the *Wall Street Journal* on August 20, 2011. It can be read here:

https://a16z.com/2011/08/20/why-software-is-eating-the-world/.

2   Wessner and Jorgenson, eds. *Measuring and Sustaining the New Economy*.

3   Leo Kelion, "Why Amazon Knows So Much About You," BBC, https://www.bbc.co.uk/news/extra/CLQYZENMBI/amazon-data.

4   Ibid.

Chapter 10

1   Pope Benedict XVI, "Caritas in Veritate" ["Charity in Truth"], June 29, 2009, https://www.vatican.va/content/benedict-xvi/en/encyclicals/documents/hf_ben-xvi_enc_20090629_caritas-in-veritate.html.

2   Alexis de Tocqueville, *Democracy in America* (first published in English in London: Sanders and Otley, 1835).

3   Jennifer Latson, "The Worst Stock Tip in History," *TIME*, September 3, 2014, https://time.com/3207128/stock-market-high-1929/.

4   John Kenneth Galbraith, *The Great Crash*, (first published by Houghton Mifflin, 1955).

Chapter 11

1 Samuel D. Warren and Louis D. Brandeis, "The Right to Privacy," *Harvard Law Review* 4, no. 5 (December 15, 1890): 193. https://www.jstor.org/stable/1321160#metadata_info_tab_contents.

2 On this subject, see Irwin R. Kramer, "The Birth of Privacy Law: A Century Since Warren and Brandeis," *Catholic University Law Review* 39, no. 3 (Spring 1990), passim.

3 David T. Kearns and David A. Nadler, *Prophets in the Dark* (New York: Harper Collins, 1992), 15; David Owen, *Copies in Seconds* (New York: Simon & Schuster, 2004), 70; Alfred Dinsdale, "Chester F. Carlson, Inventor of Xerography—A Biography," *Photographic Science and Engineering* 7 (1963): 1–4. https://classic.lib.rochester.edu/carlson/chester/biography.

4 Owen, *Copies in Seconds*, 89.

5 Personal recollection. (I used to work at Xerox.)

6 Alan F. Westin, *Privacy and Freedom* (New York: Atheneum, 1967), 7.

7 Sarah D. Scalet, "Privacy Q&A: Alan Westin on Protecting Corporate Data," *CIO*, June 15, 2003, https://www.cio.com/article/267145/security-privacy-privacy-q-a-alan-westin-on-protecting-corporate-data.html; for Tom,

the significance of this issue is enhanced by the fact that his father, Sir Michael Tugendhat, later published a similar study in the UK: *The Law of Privacy and The Media* (Oxford: Oxford University Press, 2002).

8 Simson Garfinkel, *Database Nation* (Sebastopol, CA: O'Reilly Media, 2000), 7.

9 Laurel Wamsley, "Google Says It Will No Longer Read Users' Emails to Sell Targeted Ads," June 26, 2017, NPR, https://www.npr.org/sections/thetwo-way/2017/06/26/534451513/google-says-it-will-no-longer-read-users-emails-to-sell-targeted-ads.

10 Galbraith, *The New Industrial State*.

11 Conor Friedersdorf, "Secrecy Has Already Corroded Our Democracy in Real Ways," *Atlantic*, August 8, 2013, https://www.theatlantic.com/politics/archive/2013/08/secrecy-has-already-corroded-our-democracy-in-realways/278478/.

Chapter 13

1 Stephen Bush, "Algorithms Are Here to Stay, but Ministers Must Understand Them," *Times*, August 17, 2020: https://www.thetimes.co.uk/edition/comment/algorithms-arehere-to-stay-to-but-ministers-must-understand-them-vjkwcrs0k.

Chapter 14

1 William Makepeace Thackeray, "Roundabout Papers," first published in *Cornhill Magazine*, 1860, https://www.gutenberg.org/files/2608/2608-h/2608-h.htm.

2 Galbraith, *The New Industrial State*; Francis Fukuyama, *The End of History and The Last Man* (first published by Free Press, 1992).

3 Galbraith, *The New Industrial State*.